Mometrix
TEST PREPARATION

Product ID: SSCSTG5Sci

California
Standards Tests
Grade 5 Science
Success Strategies

DEAR FUTURE EXAM SUCCESS STORY

First of all, **THANK YOU** for purchasing Mometrix study materials!

Second, congratulations! You are one of the few determined test-takers who are committed to doing whatever it takes to excel on your exam. **You have come to the right place.** We developed these study materials with one goal in mind: to deliver you the information you need in a format that's concise and easy to use.

In addition to optimizing your guide for the content of the test, we've outlined our recommended steps for breaking down the preparation process into small, attainable goals so you can make sure you stay on track.

We've also analyzed the entire test-taking process, identifying the most common pitfalls and showing how you can overcome them and be ready for any curveball the test throws you.

Standardized testing is one of the biggest obstacles on your road to success, which only increases the importance of doing well in the high-pressure, high-stakes environment of test day. Your results on this test could have a significant impact on your future, and this guide provides the information and practical advice to help you achieve your full potential on test day.

Your success is our success

We would love to hear from you! If you would like to share the story of your exam success or if you have any questions or comments in regard to our products, please contact us at **800-673-8175** or **support@mometrix.com**.

Thanks again for your business and we wish you continued success!

Sincerely,
The Mometrix Test Preparation Team

TABLE OF CONTENTS

Introduction

Thank you for purchasing this resource! You have made the choice to prepare yourself for a test that could have a huge impact on your future, and this guide is designed to help you be fully ready for test day. Obviously, it's important to have a solid understanding of the test material, but you also need to be prepared for the unique environment and stressors of the test, so that you can perform to the best of your abilities.

For this purpose, the first section that appears in this guide is the **Success Strategies**. We've devoted countless hours to meticulously researching what works and what doesn't, and we've boiled down our findings to the five most impactful steps you can take to improve your performance on the test. We start at the beginning with study planning and move through the preparation process, all the way to the testing strategies that will help you get the most out of what you know when you're finally sitting in front of the test.

We recommend that you start preparing for your test as far in advance as possible. However, if you've bought this guide as a last-minute study resource and only have a few days before your test, we recommend that you skip over the first two Success Strategies since they address a long-term study plan.

If you struggle with **test anxiety**, we strongly encourage you to check out our recommendations for how you can overcome it. Test anxiety is a formidable foe, but it can be beaten, and we want to make sure you have the tools you need to defeat it.

1

Strategy #1 – Plan Big, Study Small

There's a lot riding on your performance. If you want to ace this test, you're going to need to keep your skills sharp and the material fresh in your mind. You need a plan that lets you review everything you need to know while still fitting in your schedule. We'll break this strategy down into three categories.

Information Organization

Start with the information you already have: the official test outline. From this, you can make a complete list of all the concepts you need to cover before the test. Organize these concepts into groups that can be studied together, and create a list of any related vocabulary you need to learn so you can brush up on any difficult terms. You'll want to keep this vocabulary list handy once you actually start studying since you may need to add to it along the way.

Time Management

Once you have your set of study concepts, decide how to spread them out over the time you have left before the test. Break your study plan into small, clear goals so you have a manageable task for each day and know exactly what you're doing. Then just focus on one small step at a time. When you manage your time this way, you don't need to spend hours at a time studying. Studying a small block of content for a short period each day helps you retain information better and avoid stressing over how much you have left to do. You can relax knowing that you have a plan to cover everything in time. In order for this strategy to be effective though, you have to start studying early and stick to your schedule. Avoid the exhaustion and futility that comes from last-minute cramming!

Study Environment

The environment you study in has a big impact on your learning. Studying in a coffee shop, while probably more enjoyable, is not likely to be as fruitful as studying in a quiet room. It's important to keep distractions to a minimum. You're only planning to study for a short block of time, so make the most of it. Don't pause to check your phone or get up to find a snack. It's also important to **avoid multitasking**. Research has consistently shown that multitasking will make your studying dramatically less effective. Your study area should also be comfortable and well-lit so you don't have the distraction of straining your eyes or sitting on an uncomfortable chair.

 The time of day you study is also important. You want to be rested and alert. Don't wait until just before bedtime. Study when you'll be most likely to comprehend and remember. Even better, if you know what time of day your test will be, set that time aside for study. That way your brain will be used to working on that subject at that specific time and you'll have a better chance of recalling information.

Finally, it can be helpful to team up with others who are studying for the same test. Your actual studying should be done in as isolated an environment as possible, but the work of organizing the information and setting up the study plan can be divided up. In between study sessions, you can discuss with your teammates the concepts that you're all studying and quiz each other on the details. Just be sure that your teammates are as serious about the test as you are. If you find that your study time is being replaced with social time, you might need to find a new team.

Strategy #2 – Make Your Studying Count

You're devoting a lot of time and effort to preparing for this test, so you want to be absolutely certain it will pay off. This means doing more than just reading the content and hoping you can remember it on test day. It's important to make every minute of study count. There are two main areas you can focus on to make your studying count.

Retention

It doesn't matter how much time you study if you can't remember the material. You need to make sure you are retaining the concepts. To check your retention of the information you're learning, try recalling it at later times with minimal prompting. Try carrying around flashcards and glance at one or two from time to time or ask a friend who's also studying for the test to quiz you.

To enhance your retention, look for ways to put the information into practice so that you can apply it rather than simply recalling it. If you're using the information in practical ways, it will be much easier to remember. Similarly, it helps to solidify a concept in your mind if you're not only reading it to yourself but also explaining it to someone else. Ask a friend to let you teach them about a concept you're a little shaky on (or speak aloud to an imaginary audience if necessary). As you try to summarize, define, give examples, and answer your friend's questions, you'll understand the concepts better and they will stay with you longer. Finally, step back for a big picture view and ask yourself how each piece of information fits with the whole subject. When you link the different concepts together and see them working together as a whole, it's easier to remember the individual components.

Finally, practice showing your work on any multi-step problems, even if you're just studying. Writing out each step you take to solve a problem will help solidify the process in your mind, and you'll be more likely to remember it during the test.

Modality

Modality simply refers to the means or method by which you study. Choosing a study modality that fits your own individual learning style is crucial. No two people learn best in exactly the same way, so it's important to know your strengths and use them to your advantage.

For example, if you learn best by visualization, focus on visualizing a concept in your mind and draw an image or a diagram. Try color-coding your notes, illustrating them, or creating symbols that will trigger your mind to recall a learned concept. If you learn best by hearing or discussing information, find a study partner who learns the same way or read aloud to yourself. Think about how to put the information in your own words. Imagine that you are giving a lecture on the topic and record yourself so you can listen to it later.

For any learning style, flashcards can be helpful. Organize the information so you can take advantage of spare moments to review. Underline key words or phrases. Use different colors for different categories. Mnemonic devices (such as creating a short list in which every item starts with the same letter) can also help with retention. Find what works best for you and use it to store the information in your mind most effectively and easily.

Strategy #3 – Practice the Right Way

Your success on test day depends not only on how many hours you put into preparing, but also on whether you prepared the right way. It's good to check along the way to see if your studying is paying off. One of the most effective ways to do this is by taking practice tests to evaluate your progress. Practice tests are useful because they show exactly where you need to improve. Every time you take a practice test, pay special attention to these three groups of questions:

- The questions you got wrong
- The questions you had to guess on, even if you guessed right
- The questions you found difficult or slow to work through

This will show you exactly what your weak areas are, and where you need to devote more study time. Ask yourself why each of these questions gave you trouble. Was it because you didn't understand the material? Was it because you didn't remember the vocabulary? Do you need more repetitions on this type of question to build speed and confidence? Dig into those questions and figure out how you can strengthen your weak areas as you go back to review the material.

 Additionally, many practice tests have a section explaining the answer choices. It can be tempting to read the explanation and think that you now have a good understanding of the concept. However, an explanation likely only covers part of the question's broader context. Even if the explanation makes perfect sense, **go back and investigate** every concept related to the question until you're positive you have a thorough understanding.

As you go along, keep in mind that the practice test is just that: practice. Memorizing these questions and answers will not be very helpful on the actual test because it is unlikely to have any of the same exact questions. If you only know the right answers to the sample questions, you won't be prepared for the real thing. **Study the concepts** until you understand them fully, and then you'll be able to answer any question that shows up on the test.

It's important to wait on the practice tests until you're ready. If you take a test on your first day of study, you may be overwhelmed by the amount of material covered and how much you need to learn. Work up to it gradually.

On test day, you'll need to be prepared for answering questions, managing your time, and using the test-taking strategies you've learned. It's a lot to balance, like a mental marathon that will have a big impact on your future. Like training for a marathon, you'll need to start slowly and work your way up. When test day arrives, you'll be ready.

Start with the strategies you've read in the first two Success Strategies—plan your course and study in the way that works best for you. If you have time, consider using multiple study resources to get different approaches to the same concepts. It can be helpful to see difficult concepts from more than one angle. Then find a good source for practice tests. Many times, the test website will suggest potential study resources or provide sample tests.

Practice Test Strategy

If you're able to find at least three practice tests, we recommend this strategy:

UNTIMED AND OPEN-BOOK PRACTICE

Take the first test with no time constraints and with your notes and study guide handy. Take your time and focus on applying the strategies you've learned.

TIMED AND OPEN-BOOK PRACTICE

Take the second practice test open-book as well, but set a timer and practice pacing yourself to finish in time.

TIMED AND CLOSED-BOOK PRACTICE

Take any other practice tests as if it were test day. Set a timer and put away your study materials. Sit at a table or desk in a quiet room, imagine yourself at the testing center, and answer questions as quickly and accurately as possible.

Keep repeating timed and closed-book tests on a regular basis until you run out of practice tests or it's time for the actual test. Your mind will be ready for the schedule and stress of test day, and you'll be able to focus on recalling the material you've learned.

Strategy #4 – Pace Yourself

Once you're fully prepared for the material on the test, your biggest challenge on test day will be managing your time. Just knowing that the clock is ticking can make you panic even if you have plenty of time left. Work on pacing yourself so you can build confidence against the time constraints of the exam. Pacing is a difficult skill to master, especially in a high-pressure environment, so **practice is vital**.

Set time expectations for your pace based on how much time is available. For example, if a section has 60 questions and the time limit is 30 minutes, you know you have to average 30 seconds or less per question in order to answer them all. Although 30 seconds is the hard limit, set 25 seconds per question as your goal, so you reserve extra time to spend on harder questions. When you budget extra time for the harder questions, you no longer have any reason to stress when those questions take longer to answer.

Don't let this time expectation distract you from working through the test at a calm, steady pace, but keep it in mind so you don't spend too much time on any one question. Recognize that taking extra time on one question you don't understand may keep you from answering two that you do understand later in the test. If your time limit for a question is up and you're still not sure of the answer, mark it and move on, and come back to it later if the time and the test format allow. If the testing format doesn't allow you to return to earlier questions, just make an educated guess; then put it out of your mind and move on.

On the easier questions, be careful not to rush. It may seem wise to hurry through them so you have more time for the challenging ones, but it's not worth missing one if you know the concept and just didn't take the time to read the question fully. Work efficiently but make sure you understand the question and have looked at all of the answer choices, since more than one may seem right at first.

Even if you're paying attention to the time, you may find yourself a little behind at some point. You should speed up to get back on track, but do so wisely. Don't panic; just take a few seconds less on each question until you're caught up. Don't guess without thinking, but do look through the answer choices and eliminate any you know are wrong. If you can get down to two choices, it is often worthwhile to guess from those. Once you've chosen an answer, move on and don't dwell on any that you skipped or had to hurry through. If a question was taking too long, chances are it was one of the harder ones, so you weren't as likely to get it right anyway.

On the other hand, if you find yourself getting ahead of schedule, it may be beneficial to slow down a little. The more quickly you work, the more likely you are to make a careless mistake that will affect your score. You've budgeted time for each question, so don't be afraid to spend that time. Practice an efficient but careful pace to get the most out of the time you have.

Test-Taking Strategies

This section contains a list of test-taking strategies that you may find helpful as you work through the test. By taking what you know and applying logical thought, you can maximize your chances of answering any question correctly!

It is very important to realize that every question is different and every person is different: no single strategy will work on every question, and no single strategy will work for every person. That's why we've included all of them here, so you can try them out and determine which ones work best for different types of questions and which ones work best for you.

Question Strategies

⊘ READ CAREFULLY

Read the question and the answer choices carefully. Don't miss the question because you misread the terms. You have plenty of time to read each question thoroughly and make sure you understand what is being asked. Yet a happy medium must be attained, so don't waste too much time. You must read carefully and efficiently.

⊘ CONTEXTUAL CLUES

Look for contextual clues. If the question includes a word you are not familiar with, look at the immediate context for some indication of what the word might mean. Contextual clues can often give you all the information you need to decipher the meaning of an unfamiliar word. Even if you can't determine the meaning, you may be able to narrow down the possibilities enough to make a solid guess at the answer to the question.

⊘ PREFIXES

If you're having trouble with a word in the question or answer choices, try dissecting it. Take advantage of every clue that the word might include. Prefixes and suffixes can be a huge help. Usually, they allow you to determine a basic meaning. *Pre-* means before, *post-* means after, *pro-* is positive, *de-* is negative. From prefixes and suffixes, you can get an idea of the general meaning of the word and try to put it into context.

⊘ HEDGE WORDS

Watch out for critical hedge words, such as *likely, may, can, sometimes, often, almost, mostly, usually, generally, rarely,* and *sometimes*. Question writers insert these hedge phrases to cover every possibility. Often an answer choice will be wrong simply because it leaves no room for exception. Be on guard for answer choices that have definitive words such as *exactly* and *always*.

⊘ SWITCHBACK WORDS

Stay alert for *switchbacks*. These are the words and phrases frequently used to alert you to shifts in thought. The most common switchback words are *but, although,* and *however*. Others include *nevertheless, on the other hand, even though, while, in spite of, despite,* and *regardless of*. Switchback words are important to catch because they can change the direction of the question or an answer choice.

7

⊘ Face Value

When in doubt, use common sense. Accept the situation in the problem at face value. Don't read too much into it. These problems will not require you to make wild assumptions. If you have to go beyond creativity and warp time or space in order to have an answer choice fit the question, then you should move on and consider the other answer choices. These are normal problems rooted in reality. The applicable relationship or explanation may not be readily apparent, but it is there for you to figure out. Use your common sense to interpret anything that isn't clear.

Answer Choice Strategies

⊘ Answer Selection

The most thorough way to pick an answer choice is to identify and eliminate wrong answers until only one is left, then confirm it is the correct answer. Sometimes an answer choice may immediately seem right, but be careful. The test writers will usually put more than one reasonable answer choice on each question, so take a second to read all of them and make sure that the other choices are not equally obvious. As long as you have time left, it is better to read every answer choice than to pick the first one that looks right without checking the others.

⊘ Answer Choice Families

An answer choice family consists of two (in rare cases, three) answer choices that are very similar in construction and cannot all be true at the same time. If you see two answer choices that are direct opposites or parallels, one of them is usually the correct answer. For instance, if one answer choice says that quantity x increases and another either says that quantity x decreases (opposite) or says that quantity y increases (parallel), then those answer choices would fall into the same family. An answer choice that doesn't match the construction of the answer choice family is more likely to be incorrect. Most questions will not have answer choice families, but when they do appear, you should be prepared to recognize them.

⊘ Eliminate Answers

Eliminate answer choices as soon as you realize they are wrong, but make sure you consider all possibilities. If you are eliminating answer choices and realize that the last one you are left with is also wrong, don't panic. Start over and consider each choice again. There may be something you missed the first time that you will realize on the second pass.

⊘ Avoid Fact Traps

Don't be distracted by an answer choice that is factually true but doesn't answer the question. You are looking for the choice that answers the question. Stay focused on what the question is asking for so you don't accidentally pick an answer that is true but incorrect. Always go back to the question and make sure the answer choice you've selected actually answers the question and is not merely a true statement.

⊘ Extreme Statements

In general, you should avoid answers that put forth extreme actions as standard practice or proclaim controversial ideas as established fact. An answer choice that states the "process should be used in certain situations, if..." is much more likely to be correct than one that states the "process should be discontinued completely." The first is a calm rational statement and doesn't even make a definitive, uncompromising stance, using a hedge word *if* to provide wiggle room, whereas the second choice is far more extreme.

8

⊘ Benchmark

As you read through the answer choices and you come across one that seems to answer the question well, mentally select that answer choice. This is not your final answer, but it's the one that will help you evaluate the other answer choices. The one that you selected is your benchmark or standard for judging each of the other answer choices. Every other answer choice must be compared to your benchmark. That choice is correct until proven otherwise by another answer choice beating it. If you find a better answer, then that one becomes your new benchmark. Once you've decided that no other choice answers the question as well as your benchmark, you have your final answer.

⊘ Predict the Answer

Before you even start looking at the answer choices, it is often best to try to predict the answer. When you come up with the answer on your own, it is easier to avoid distractions and traps because you will know exactly what to look for. The right answer choice is unlikely to be word-for-word what you came up with, but it should be a close match. Even if you are confident that you have the right answer, you should still take the time to read each option before moving on.

General Strategies

⊘ Tough Questions

If you are stumped on a problem or it appears too hard or too difficult, don't waste time. Move on! Remember though, if you can quickly check for obviously incorrect answer choices, your chances of guessing correctly are greatly improved. Before you completely give up, at least try to knock out a couple of possible answers. Eliminate what you can and then guess at the remaining answer choices before moving on.

⊘ Check Your Work

Since you will probably not know every term listed and the answer to every question, it is important that you get credit for the ones that you do know. Don't miss any questions through careless mistakes. If at all possible, try to take a second to look back over your answer selection and make sure you've selected the correct answer choice and haven't made a costly careless mistake (such as marking an answer choice that you didn't mean to mark). This quick double check should more than pay for itself in caught mistakes for the time it costs.

⊘ Pace Yourself

It's easy to be overwhelmed when you're looking at a page full of questions; your mind is confused and full of random thoughts, and the clock is ticking down faster than you would like. Calm down and maintain the pace that you have set for yourself. Especially as you get down to the last few minutes of the test, don't let the small numbers on the clock make you panic. As long as you are on track by monitoring your pace, you are guaranteed to have time for each question.

⊘ Don't Rush

It is very easy to make errors when you are in a hurry. Maintaining a fast pace in answering questions is pointless if it makes you miss questions that you would have gotten right otherwise. Test writers like to include distracting information and wrong answers that seem right. Taking a little extra time to avoid careless mistakes can make all the difference in your test score. Find a pace that allows you to be confident in the answers that you select.

⊘ Keep Moving

Panicking will not help you pass the test, so do your best to stay calm and keep moving. Taking deep breaths and going through the answer elimination steps you practiced can help to break through a stress barrier and keep your pace.

Final Notes

The combination of a solid foundation of content knowledge and the confidence that comes from practicing your plan for applying that knowledge is the key to maximizing your performance on test day. As your foundation of content knowledge is built up and strengthened, you'll find that the strategies included in this chapter become more and more effective in helping you quickly sift through the distractions and traps of the test to isolate the correct answer.

Now that you're preparing to move forward into the test content chapters of this book, be sure to keep your goal in mind. As you read, think about how you will be able to apply this information on the test. If you've already seen sample questions for the test and you have an idea of the question format and style, try to come up with questions of your own that you can answer based on what you're reading. This will give you valuable practice applying your knowledge in the same ways you can expect to on test day.

Good luck and good studying!

Science

Scientific Investigation and Reasoning

SAFETY PROCEDURES

Everyone working in a lab setting should be careful to follow these rules to protect themselves and others from injury or accidents.

- Students should wear a **lab apron** and **safety goggles**.
- **Loose** or **dangling** clothing and jewelry, necklaces, and earrings should not be worn.
- Those with **long hair** should tie it back.
- Care should always be taken not to **splash chemicals**.
- **Open-toed shoes** such as sandals and flip-flops should not be worn, nor should wrist watches.
- **Glasses** are preferable to contact lenses since the latter carries a risk of chemicals getting caught between the lens and the eye.
- Students should always be **supervised** during an experiment.
- The area where the experiment is taking place and the surrounding floor should be **free of clutter**.
- **Food** and **drink** should also not be allowed in a lab setting.
- **Cords** should not be allowed to **dangle** from work stations.
- There should be no **rough-housing** in the lab.
- **Wash hands** before and after the lab is complete.

SAFETY GLOVES

There are many types of **gloves** available to help protect the skin from cuts, burns, and chemical splashes. There are many considerations to take into account when choosing a glove. For example, gloves that are highly protective may limit grip or accuracy. Some gloves may not offer appropriate protection against a specific chemical. Disposable latex, vinyl, or nitrile gloves are usually appropriate for most circumstances, and offer protection from incidental splashes and contact.

LABORATORY ACCIDENTS

Accidents happen in labs, so it is important to know how to clean up, stay safe, and report the accident to the teacher. Any spills or accidents should be **reported** to the teacher so that the teacher can determine the safest clean-up method. The student should start to wash off a **chemical** spilled on the skin while reporting the incident. Some spills may require removal of contaminated clothing and use of the **safety shower**. Broken glass should be disposed of in a designated container. If someone's clothing catches fire they should walk to the safety shower and use it to extinguish the flames. A fire blanket may be used to smother a **lab fire**. A fire extinguisher, phone, spill neutralizers, and a first aid box are other types of **safety equipment** found in the lab. Students should be familiar with **routes** out of the room and the building in case of fire.

NATURAL RESOURCES, RENEWABLE RESOURCES, NONRENEWABLE RESOURCES, AND COMMODITIES

Natural resources are things provided by nature that have value to humans, such as minerals, energy, timber, fish, wildlife, and the landscape. **Renewable resources** are those that can be replenished, such as wind, solar radiation, tides, and water (with proper conservation and clean-

11

up). Soil is renewable with proper conservation and management techniques, and timber can be replenished with replanting. Living resources such as fish and wildlife can replenish themselves if they are not over-harvested. **Nonrenewable resources** are those that cannot be replenished. These include fossil fuels such as oil and coal and metal ores. These cannot be replaced or reused once they have been burned, although some of their products can be recycled. **Commodities** are natural resources that have to be extracted and purified rather than created, such as mineral ores.

RECYCLING AND PROTECTING THE ENVIRONMENT

When trash is thrown away without separating it out for recycling, it usually goes to a landfill where it cannot be recovered and reused. Metal and plastic do not break down readily, and by sending those to the general trash, those materials are essentially lost. Aluminum cans, like soda cans and canned foods can be recycled and used to make new products down the line. The same can be said of most paper and plastics. Recycling bins are usually next to normal trash cans and have the recycle symbol marked on it. This is usually three arrows pointing at each other in a triangle:

DEFINITION OF SCIENCE

Scientific knowledge is knowledge about the world that we understand by observing and testing. The **scientific process** is how we try to gain scientific knowledge. The steps are to make an initial observation, make a hypothesis, test the hypothesis with an experiment, draw conclusions from the experiment, then start over with new observations.

OBSERVATIONS

An **observation** is something specific you notice about the world or an event. For instance, a very obvious event that takes place is if we leave milk out on the counter overnight, the milk will go bad. We observe this event by using our five senses: sight, taste, smell, touch, and sound. When milk goes bad, there are several ways it changes.

HYPOTHESIS

The next step of the scientific process is to make an educated guess about what might happen in a certain event. This is also known as a **hypothesis**. A hypothesis about milk might be that if I keep milk above a certain temperature for a long time, it will go bad. Hypotheses need to be specific and testable so we can decide if it is true or false.

EXPERIMENT

The step after making a hypothesis is to check if it is true by testing it with an **experiment**. Experiments need to be a controlled, specific situation that tells us if our educated guess was correct. Experiments need to ask questions about **facts**, rather than **opinions**. Usually, the more specific the experiment, the clearer the answer will be. For instance, if I test my hypothesis by putting milk outside overnight, but do not set a timer, then I can get an answer, but I will not be able to record how time affected the experiment. Similarly, if the milk is outside and the temperature changes overnight, I will not be able to learn much about what effect the temperature had on the milk.

VARIABLES

These two aspects of the experiment are examples of variables. **Variables** are parts of the experiment that can change. Some variables are controlled, while others are aspects that we observe. For instance, we cannot control time, but we can observe the milk over time by checking it every half hour. Temperature, on the other hand, can be controlled with technology. We can keep the milk inside the house, where the temperature will always be around 70 degrees, or we can keep it in the refrigerator, where the milk will stay close to 40 degrees. These variables need to be controlled as best as possible to get the most specific results.

REPEATING EXPERIMENTS

Experiments should be **repeated** to see if the same result happens every time. For example, if you can get the same result only three out of ten attempts, then the result is not reliable and the experiment should be changed and tried again. Another example is that if you are testing how milk changes by setting it out, try changing the temperature each time to see if the same result happens at different temperatures.

REFLECT

After an experiment is complete, the scientist needs to **reflect** on what happened by asking questions:

- Did the experiment answer the question?
- Was the hypothesis true or false?
- Did repeated attempts produce the same results?
- Is there anything I should change for future attempts?
- What did I learn?
- What questions can I ask now that I have learned something?

REPEAT THE PROCESS

After the experiment and reflection is over, the scientist hopefully learned something and can ask new questions. These questions should be more specific, or the experiment should be improved to get better answers.

OBSERVED AND MEASURED DATA

Data can be either measurable or observable. **Observable data** is often referred to as **qualitative data**, because it describes specific **qualities** of something being observed. An example of this is color or smell. It is very difficult to find numbers to describe a color or smell, but it is not hard to describe that a liquid changed from red to blue. **Measurable data** is also known as **quantitative data** because it refers to the quantity or amount of something. A good example of quantitative data is weight. Any time someone steps on a scale to know how much they weigh, they are looking at quantitative data. Both types of data are important to keep track of and record.

METRIC SYSTEM

The **metric system** is the accepted standard of measurement in the scientific community. **Standardization** is helpful because it allows the results of experiments to be compared and reproduced without the need to laboriously convert measurements. Metric system uses similar conversions between all types of measurement, including length, mass, volume, time, and temperature.

ENGLISH AND METRIC (SCIENTIFIC) UNITS OF MEASUREMENT

The English system commonly used in the United States is not based on consistent smaller units. Thus, 12 inches equal 1 foot, 3 feet equal 1 yard, and 5,280 feet equal 1 mile. The metric system used in science and most countries of the world is based on units of 10. Therefore, 1000 millimeters and 100 centimeters equal 1 meter, and 1,000 meters equal a kilometer. The same pattern is true for the other units of measurement in the two systems. The following table shows the different units.

Unit	English System	Metric System
length	inch, foot, mile	centimeter, meter, kilometer
mass, weight	net weight ounce, pound	gram, kilogram, newton
volume	fluid ounce, pint, quart	milliliter, liter
temperature	Fahrenheit degree	Celsius degree

FAHRENHEIT AND CELSIUS TEMPERATURE SCALES

In the Fahrenheit scale the point where water freezes and ice melts is set at 32°, and the point where water boils and water vapor condenses is 212°. That means a difference of 180° between the freezing and boiling points of water. In the Celsius scale, the freezing/melting point is set at 0°and the boiling/condensation point at 100°, making this scale much easier to use.

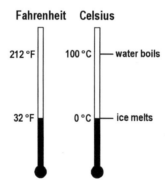

BASIC UNITS OF MEASUREMENT

METRIC SYSTEM

The metric system is generally accepted as the preferred method for taking measurements. Having a universal standard allows individuals to interpret measurements more easily, regardless of where they are located.

The basic units of measurement are: the **meter**, which measures length; the **liter**, which measures volume; and the **gram**, which measures mass. The metric system starts with a **base unit** and increases or decreases in units of 10. The prefix and the base unit combined are used to indicate an amount.

14

For example, deka is 10 times the base unit. A dekameter is 10 meters; a dekaliter is 10 liters; and a dekagram is 10 grams. The prefix hecto refers to 100 times the base amount; kilo is 1,000 times the base amount. The prefixes that indicate a fraction of the base unit are deci, which is 1/10 of the base unit; centi, which is 1/100 of the base unit; and milli, which is 1/1000 of the base unit.

> **Review Video: Metric System Conversions**
> Visit mometrix.com/academy and enter code: 163709

COMMON PREFIXES

The prefixes for **multiples** are as follows:

- **deka** (da), 10 (deka is the American spelling, but deca is also used)
- **hecto** (h), 100
- **kilo** (k), 1000
- **mega** (M), 100,000

The prefixes for **subdivisions** are as follows:

- **deci** (d), 1/10
- **centi** (c), 1/100
- **milli** (m), 1/1000
- **micro** (μ), 1/100,000

VENN DIAGRAMS

One helpful way of sorting out information when comparing two things is a **venn diagram.** This tool is essentially just two circles that overlap, and it is used to display what aspects of one thing are similar or different from another thing. In the following diagram, notice how fish and frogs are similar in some ways, but different in others.

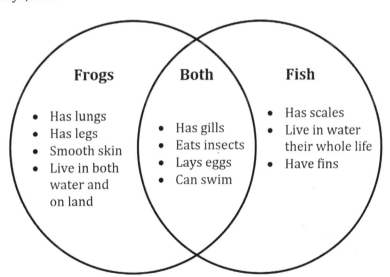

FREQUENCY TABLES

Frequency tables show how frequently each unique value appears in a set. A **relative frequency table** is one that shows the proportions of each unique value compared to the entire set. Relative frequencies are given as percentages; however, the total percent for a relative frequency table will not necessarily equal 100 percent due to rounding. An example of a frequency table with relative frequencies is below.

Favorite Color	Frequency	Relative Frequency
Blue	4	13%
Red	7	22%
Green	3	9%
Purple	6	19%
Cyan	12	38%

CIRCLE GRAPHS

Circle graphs, also known as *pie charts*, provide a visual depiction of the relationship of each type of data compared to the whole set of data. The circle graph is divided into sections by drawing radii to create central angles whose percentage of the circle is equal to the individual data's percentage of the whole set. Each 1% of data is equal to 3.6° in the circle graph. Therefore, data represented by a 90° section of the circle graph makes up 25% of the whole. When complete, a circle graph often looks like a pie cut into uneven wedges. The pie chart below shows the data from the frequency table referenced earlier where people were asked their favorite color.

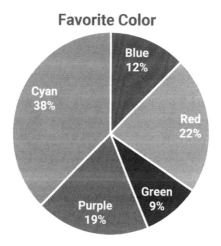

PICTOGRAPHS

A **pictograph** is a graph, generally in the horizontal orientation, that uses pictures or symbols to represent the data. Each pictograph must have a key that defines the picture or symbol and gives the quantity each picture or symbol represents. Pictures or symbols on a pictograph are not always shown as whole elements. In this case, the fraction of the picture or symbol shown represents the same fraction of the quantity a whole picture or symbol stands for. For example, a row with $3\frac{1}{2}$ ears of corn, where each ear of corn represents 100 stalks of corn in a field, would equal $3\frac{1}{2} \times 100 = 350$ stalks of corn in the field.

LINE GRAPHS

Line graphs have one or more lines of varying styles (solid or broken) to show the different values for a set of data. The individual data are represented as ordered pairs, much like on a Cartesian plane. In this case, the x- and y-axes are defined in terms of their units, such as dollars or time. The individual plotted points are joined by line segments to show whether the value of the data is increasing (line sloping upward), decreasing (line sloping downward), or staying the same

16

(horizontal line). Multiple sets of data can be graphed on the same line graph to give an easy visual comparison. An example of this would be graphing achievement test scores for different groups of students over the same time period to see which group had the greatest increase or decrease in performance from year to year (as shown below).

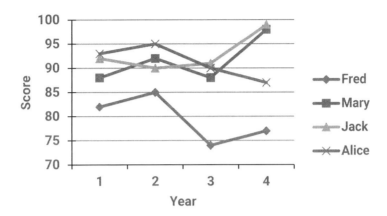

LINE PLOTS

A **line plot**, also known as a *dot plot*, has plotted points that are not connected by line segments. In this graph, the horizontal axis lists the different possible values for the data, and the vertical axis lists the number of times the individual value occurs. A single dot is graphed for each value to show the number of times it occurs. This graph is more closely related to a bar graph than a line graph. Do not connect the dots in a line plot or it will misrepresent the data.

STEM AND LEAF PLOTS

A **stem and leaf plot** is useful for depicting groups of data that fall into a range of values. Each piece of data is separated into two parts: the first, or left, part is called the stem; the second, or right, part is called the leaf. Each stem is listed in a column from smallest to largest. Each leaf that has the common stem is listed in that stem's row from smallest to largest. For example, in a set of two-digit numbers, the digit in the tens place is the stem, and the digit in the ones place is the leaf. With a stem and leaf plot, you can easily see which subset of numbers (10s, 20s, 30s, etc.) is the largest. This information is also readily available by looking at a histogram, but a stem and leaf plot also allows you to look closer and see exactly which values fall in that range. Using all of the test scores from above, we can assemble a stem and leaf plot like the one below.

Test Scores

7	4 8
8	2 5 7 8 8
9	0 0 1 2 2 3 5 8 9

BAR GRAPHS

A **bar graph** is one of the few graphs that can be drawn correctly in two different configurations – both horizontally and vertically. A bar graph is similar to a line plot in the way the data is organized on the graph. Both axes must have their categories defined for the graph to be useful. Rather than placing a single dot to mark the point of the data's value, a bar, or thick line, is drawn from zero to the exact value of the data, whether it is a number, percentage, or other numerical value. Longer bar lengths correspond to greater data values. To read a bar graph, read the labels for the axes to find the units being reported. Then, look where the bars end in relation to the scale given on the corresponding axis and determine the associated value.

The bar chart below represents the responses from our favorite-color survey.

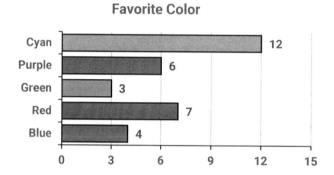

SCIENTIFIC MODELS

Scientists often create **models** to help express and understand scientific ideas. A model is a representation of an idea that is used to experience something that cannot be experienced directly. For instance, we cannot see and experience evaporation directly, but we can easily draw out the process of evaporation, condensation, and precipitation. Having a drawing helps us to understand the concept since we cannot experience it directly. Models can be three-dimensional, such as something you can hold, or they can be simple diagrams demonstrating a process. For instance, a planetarium is a large model that helps someone see the size of planets and stars and how they interact. More typical models in the classroom include baking soda and vinegar volcanoes, solar system mobiles, or molecules made from foam and straws. Other models can include a diagram showing the water cycle.

LIMITATIONS OF MODELS

Using models can be very helpful for experiencing a scientific process that normally couldn't be observed directly, but they are naturally limited. Models are usually used to express a very large thing in a small way, such as a volcano or the planet earth in a way that a human can look at it and touch it. Models are also often used to express very small things or invisible things in a more observable way. Changing the size or the materials used to express something heavily limits how effective a model is. For instance, if a model on the water cycle used cotton balls to show clouds, it impairs our understanding of clouds. Clouds are not made of dry, solid cotton, but are made up of vapor filled with water. Volcanos made from clay and that use baking soda and vinegar do not demonstrate the extreme heat or mass of volcanic materials. Similarly, a mobile of the solar system cannot express how extremely large the sun and planets are. When using a model to understand a concept, the observer needs to be aware that they are probably only getting a clear picture of one side of the concept, and not understanding it fully.

TOOLS FOR MEASURING AND OBSERVATION

Purpose	Tool
Measuring Length	Rulers, meter sticks
Measuring Weight or Mass	Spring scales, pan balances
Measuring Volume	Beakers, graduated cylinders
Measuring Time	Timers, clocks
Measuring Temperature	Thermometer
Recording Information	Journals, notebooks
Observing Animals and Plants	Terrariums, aquariums, collecting nets
Observing Weather	Rain Gauges, wind vanes,
Models for Understanding Concepts	Sun-Earth-Moon System Models, volcano models, water cycle models
Visual Observation	cameras, hand lenses, microscopes

SCIENCE CAREERS

Almost all fields require people who think like scientists or use science directly.

- **Meteorologists** – study the atmosphere to predict weather.
- **Engineers** – use physics and chemistry to design complicated technology and processes.
- **Doctors** – use biology to learn how the body and disease works.
- **Astronomers** – use physics and space science to study the Earth and the universe and travel into space.

CONTRIBUTIONS OF SCIENTISTS

- **Sir Francis Bacon** – contributed many ideas that helped develop the modern scientific method.
- **Gallileo Galilei**– one of the first people to use a telescope and contributed ideas about how gravity works. He also contributed the idea that the Earth revolved around the Sun, and not the other way around.
- **Leonardo da Vinci** – known for his contributions to art and to science, he was an avid inventor, designing a submarine, an armored tank, and several aircraft far before any of which were actually built.
- **Sir Isaac Newton** – best known for his contributions to physics. He described the principals of inertia and friction.
- **Louis Pasteur** – discovered bacteria and invented the process of pasteurization and developed some of the first vaccines.
- **Thomas Edison** – invented many distinct devices, including the phonograph, improved upon the telephone, the lightbulb, and the kinetoscope, an early form of movie projector.
- **Albert Einstein** – studied theoretical physics with the use of mathematics and is particularly famous for his theory of relativity

Matter and Energy

INTENSIVE AND EXTENSIVE PHYSICAL PROPERTIES OF MATTER

Intensive properties are those that do not depend upon the size of the sample. Examples are density, melting-freezing point, boiling point, color, chemical reactivity, luster, malleability, and electrical conductivity. **Extensive properties** do depend on the size of the sample. Examples include the amount of space occupied (volume), mass, and weight. Note that mass and weight are not the same thing. Mass is the amount of material present in a body, whereas weight is the gravitational force acting upon that mass in a specific gravitational field. A 100-kilogram object has the same mass on Earth as on the Moon, but its weight will change markedly. It will weigh 980.7 Newtons (220.5 pounds) here on Earth, but only 163.5 N (36.75 lbs) on the Moon. In outer space this object would weigh nothing at all, but would still have a mass of 100 kg.

PROPERTIES OF MATTER

Matter is anything that takes up space and has weight. Even air has weight and takes up space. All types of matter have different properties that can be observed or measured. There are many properties of matter, including temperature, mass, magnetism, and the ability to sink or float.

TEMPERATURE

Temperature is a property that tells how hot or cold a thing is. **Temperature** also demonstrates how much **thermal energy** is in a thing. When an object is cold, it has very little thermal energy. For many substances, being hot makes the substance expand, while being cold makes it shrink. Temperature also tends to transfer from one object to another. For instance, when a cup is filled with ice and water, the ice and water exchange energy until they are the same temperature. The ice and water reach the same temperature eventually, usually resulting in the ice melting.

MASS AND WEIGHT

Mass is a measure of how much **matter** is in an object. **Mass** is usually measured by placing an object on a scale. The terms mass and weight are often used interchangeably, but they actually have different definitions. Mass is always the same for a specific object, but **weight** depends on other factors. For instance, 1,000 lb. car always has the same mass, but it would weigh different amounts depending on if the car were on Earth or on Mars, which has much lower gravity.

VOLUME AND DENSITY

Volume is a measure of the **size** of an object or how much space an object takes up. Volume affects several other factors like density. Density is the amount of **mass** (amount of matter) in a certain **volume**. The more matter there is, the more mass an object has. **Density** takes into account both the mass and volume of an object. For instance, an inflated balloon has very little mass in it, but it is fairly large. A watermelon is about the same size, but has much more mass in it, so the watermelon is denser than the balloon. Density is the reason things float or sink. One example is oil and water. Oil is usually thicker than water, but it is actually less dense. If you put oil and water in a cup, you can see that the oil always **floats** to the top. Another way of thinking about it is that the water is actually **sinking** in the oil.

DENSITY OF WATER

Density is the **mass** (amount of matter) in a certain **volume**. The more **matter** there is, the more the object weighs. Most solids have more matter than the same volume of their liquids. This means that they are denser and sink in their own liquid. However, water is different. The molecules in ice are farther apart than they are in liquid water. That means that ice has less matter in it than the same volume of liquid water. Therefore, ice is less dense and floats in water.

MATERIALS DENSER THAN WATER

Ships and other floating objects made of materials that are denser than water float because of the empty space they contain inside their hulls. A ship weighing 5,000 tons overall will displace 5,000 tons of water, but this weight of water will occupy a smaller volume than the ship itself. Once this amount of water has been displaced the ship will not sink any deeper into the water and will float. Archimedes' principle states that the buoyant force is equal to the weight of the water (or any other fluid displaced). The reason a solid piece of iron or a rock sinks is that it weighs more than the volume of water it displaces. For the same reason, because a helium-filled balloon is lighter than air it will rise until the air's density is reduced such that the volume of air displaced is the same as the volume of the balloon.

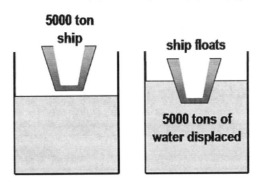

DENSITY OF WATER AND ICE

Most solids have more matter than the same volume of their liquids. This means that they are denser and sink in their own liquid. However, water is different. The molecules in ice are farther apart than they are in liquid water. That means that ice has less matter in it than the same volume of liquid water. Therefore, ice is less dense and floats in water.

MAGNETISM

Magnetism is a property that some rocks or metals can possess. **Magnetism** is a force that can push or pull on other magnetic materials. Magnets always have two poles, which attract the opposite pole and repel the same pole. Usually, the poles on a magnet are identified as being North or South, because the Earth's North and South Poles are actually magnetic as well. This is the reason that compasses work. The small needle in a compass is attracted to the Earth's poles and points in that direction. Many types of technology use magnetism, including electronics, motors, credit cards, and others.

MAGNETS

A magnet is a metal or object that produces a magnetic field. A magnetic field is mapped by invisible curved lines of force that attract magnets or certain metals like iron or nickel. A simple bar magnet has a south pole (S) at one end and a north pole (N) at the other. Each pole will attract the opposite pole of another magnet and repel the same pole. The north pole of a compass needle will point to the south pole of a magnet, while the south pole of the needle will be attracted to the north pole of the magnet.

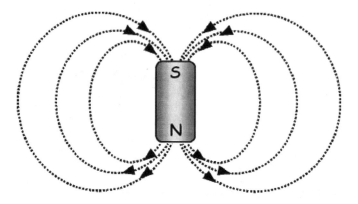

OPPOSITE POLES OF TWO MAGNETS ATTRACT EACH OTHER

When two bar magnets are lined end to end with the north and south poles near each other, the lines of force run from the north pole of one magnet to the south pole of the other magnet indicating attraction.

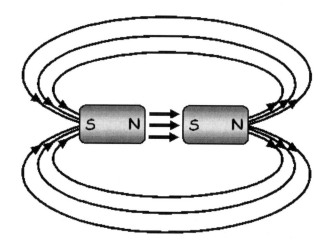

CUTTING A BAR MAGNET IN TWO

If a bar magnet is cut in two, two complete magnets will form, each with a north and south pole. If a bar magnet is cut it into three parts, three magnets will form.

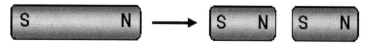

POLES OF TWO MAGNETS REPEL EACH OTHER

When the like poles of two magnets are brought close to each other the lines of force run in opposite directions. This causes the two poles to push each other away.

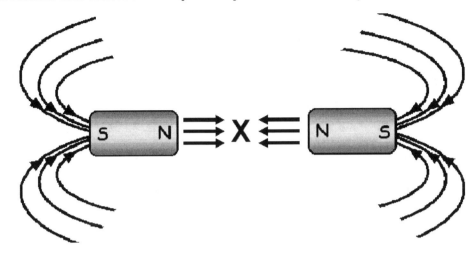

NEEDLE OF A MAGNETIC COMPASS

Planet Earth has a magnetic field just like a bar magnet. The north pole of a compass needle points to Earth's north pole because the magnetic pole near the North Pole is actually the south pole of Earth's magnetic field. Likewise, the south pole of the compass needle is attracted to the north pole of Earth's magnetic field near the south geographic pole. Just remember that each magnetic pole is attracted to its opposite pole on another magnet or magnetic object.

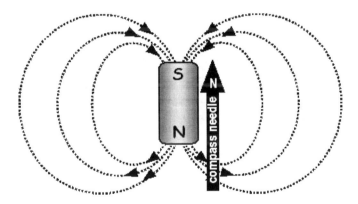

CONDUCTIVITY

Conductivity is a property that describes how easily a material **transfers energy** to and from other materials. **Conductivity** usually refers to either heat energy or electrical energy. For instance, metals are usually good at conducting both heat and electricity, whereas plastic usually is not good at conducting these types of energy. Materials that are good at transferring energy are known as **conductors**, whereas materials that are not good at transferring energy are known as **resistors**.

PHYSICAL CHANGES

Physical changes are those that do not affect the chemical properties of a substance. Changes in state are **physical changes**. For example, a liquid can freeze into a solid or boil into a gas without changing the chemical nature of the substance. It is all still the same substance. Ice, steam, and liquid water are all still water, H_2O. Physical properties include such features as shape, texture, size,

23

volume, mass, and density. Cutting, melting, dissolving, mixing, breaking, and crushing are all types of physical changes.

CHEMICAL CHANGES

Chemical changes occur when chemical bonds are broken and new ones are formed. The original substances are **transformed** into different substances. If vinegar and baking soda are mixed together, a lot of bubbles (carbon dioxide) and water will form. Burning wood in a fireplace is another type of chemical change. The carbon in the wood reacts with oxygen in the air to make ash, carbon dioxide, smoke and energy that we feel as heat and see as light.

Examples of chemical changes include the following:

- (a) The temperature of a system changes without any heating or cooling.
- (b) The formation of a gas (bubbles).
- (c) The formation of a precipitate (solid) when two liquids are mixed.
- (d) A liquid changes color.

A **chemical change** occurs when two or more substances come together and interact in such a way that they become completely new substances. For example, two hydrogen atoms and one oxygen atom combine to make a new compound—a water molecule, H_2O. Likewise, two oxygen atoms and one carbon atom combine to make one molecule of carbon dioxide—CO_2. The two substances that combine are called **reactants,** and the new compound that emerges is the **product**. Chemical reactions (changes) can be much more complicated than this.

STATES OF MATTER

The four states of matter are solid, liquid, gas, and plasma. **Solids** have a definite shape and a definite volume. Because solid particles are held in fairly rigid positions, solids are the least compressible of the four states of matter. **Liquids** have definite volumes but no definite shapes. Because their particles are free to slip and slide over each other, liquids take the shape of their containers, but they still remain fairly incompressible by natural means. **Gases** have no definite shape or volume. Because gas particles are free to move, they move away from each other to fill their containers. Gases are compressible. **Plasmas** are high-temperature, ionized gases that exist only under very high temperatures at which electrons are stripped away from their atoms.

> **Review Video: States of Matter**
> Visit mometrix.com/academy and enter code: 742449
>
> **Review Video: States of Matter [Advanced]**
> Visit mometrix.com/academy and enter code: 298130
>
> **Review Video: Properties of Liquids**
> Visit mometrix.com/academy and enter code: 802024

The following table shows similarities and differences between solids, liquids, and gases:

	Solid	Liquid	Gas
Shape	Fixed shape	No fixed shape (assumes shape of container)	No fixed shape (assumes shape of container)
Volume	Fixed	Fixed	Changes to assume shape of container
Fluidity	Does not flow easily	Flows easily	Flows easily
Compressibility	Hard to compress	Hard to compress	Compresses

SIX DIFFERENT TYPES OF PHASE CHANGE

A substance that is undergoing a change from a solid to a liquid is said to be melting. If this change occurs in the opposite direction, from liquid to solid, this change is called freezing. A liquid which is being converted to a gas is undergoing vaporization. The reverse of this process is known as condensation. Direct transitions from gas to solid and solid to gas are much less common in everyday life, but they can occur given the proper conditions. Solid to gas conversion is known as sublimation, while the reverse is called deposition.

> **Review Video: Chemical and Physical Properties of Matter**
> Visit mometrix.com/academy and enter code: 717349

STATES OF MATTER

The three states of matter are *solids*, *liquids*, and *gases*. In a **solid** the *atoms* or *molecules* of a substance are close together and locked into place. A solid has a definite shape and volume. In a liquid the atoms or molecules are farther apart. A **liquid** flows and takes the shape of its container. In a **gas** the atoms or molecules are very far apart and have a lot of energy. They will fly completely way if not held inside a container like a balloon or a closed bottle. The state of matter that a substance takes on depends mainly on temperature and pressure. For instance, candle wax is usually a solid in normal temperatures on Earth, but if it heats up, it easily melts. Paper, on the other hand, does not melt, but burns and turns directly into a gas.

Solid	Liquid	Gas
Have a definite shape and size. Usually denser than liquids and gases of the same material.	Have a definite size, but do not have a definite shape.	Does not have a definite size or shape, but matches its container.
• Rocks • Ice Cream • Pencils • Apples	• Milk • Water • Juice • Rain	• Steam • Fire • Helium • Fog

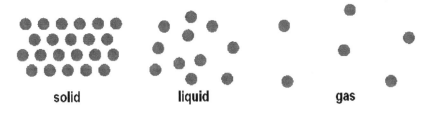

PHASE STATES OF WATER

Water has three states of matter: ice, liquid water, and water vapor. Water freezes at 32 degrees Fahrenheit, where ice crystals form and the substance becomes a solid.

- **Ice** - Water crystalizes when it freezes, which means that it actually expands when it freezes, making it less dense than liquid water. This is uncommon because solids are usually the most dense form of a substance because the atoms are more tightly compressed. That is why ice actually floats in liquid water, rather than sinks.
- **Water Vapor** – Water exists in gas form as it evaporates or boils. Water vapor exists in the air and is often referred to as humidity. There is always some moisture in the air, though as the temperatures drop or pressure changes, it will condense and become liquid water again. Just like all other gas forms, water vapor spreads out in its container and flows much like a liquid.
- **Liquid Water** – Liquid water is the most common form on Earth. Water is needed for life and makes up most of the matter in a human body. Liquid water follows all of the typical rules for liquids, including taking the shape of its container, but has a constant mass and volume.

MIXTURE, SOLUTION, AND COLLOID

A **mixture** is made of two or more substances that are combined in various proportions. The exact proportion of the constituents is the defining characteristic of any mixture. There are two types of mixtures: homogeneous and heterogeneous. **Homogeneous** means that the mixture's composition and properties are uniform throughout. Conversely, **heterogeneous** means that the mixture's composition and properties are not uniform throughout.

SOLUTIONS AND SOLUBILITY

A **solution** is a homogeneous mixture of substances that cannot be separated by filtration or centrifugation. Solutions are made by dissolving one or more solutes into a solvent. For example, in a solution of sugar and water, sugar is the solute and water is the solvent. If there is more than one liquid present in the solution, then the most prevalent liquid is considered the solvent. The exact mechanism of dissolving varies depending on the mixture, but the result is always individual solute ions or molecules surrounded by solvent molecules. The proportion of solute to solvent for a particular solution is its **concentration**. Not all materials are able to be dissolved. Sugar is considered **soluble** in water, but sand does not dissolve in water, so it is considered **insoluble** in water.

A **colloid** is a heterogeneous mixture in which small particles (<1 micrometer) are suspended, but not dissolved, in a liquid. As such, they can be separated by centrifugation. A commonplace example of a colloid is milk.

PHYSICAL PROPERTIES OF MIXTURES AND SOLUTIONS

When making a mixture or solution of ingredients, a person is not making a chemical change to the ingredients. Since the original ingredients are still present, their **physical properties** are usually still observable in the final mixture. Take, for instance, a solution of salt and water. The salt dissolves completely in the water, but since the salt is still present, the solution then tastes salty. Other properties, such as magnetism, do not transfer to the whole mixture. If a person were to mix sand and iron filings, then wave a magnet over the mixture, the iron filings would separate out, leaving only sand behind.

ACIDS AND BASES AND WATER

One property of matter is called its pH value, which determines if a chemical is an **acid** or a **base**. Acids, such as lemon juice, tend to taste sour, whereas bases, such as soap, tend to feel slippery and taste bitter. Some chemicals, such as water, are called **neutral** because they are neither an acid or a base. Just like with other mixtures of ingredients with different properties, an acid or a base can be mixed with water to change the strength of the property. Lemon juice is very strong and sour to the taste at full strength, but when mixed with water and sugar, it can be sweet instead of sour. To add water to reduce the strength of a solution is called **dilution.**

	Very Acidic			**Neutral**			**Very Basic**
pH value	0-2	2-4	5-7	7	7-9	10-12	12-14
	Hydrochloric Acid and Stomach Acid	Vinegar, Fruit Juice, and Sodas	Tomatoes and Bananas	Water	Eggs and Baking Soda	Soap and Ammonia	Bleach and Drain Cleaner

Force, Motion, and Energy

TYPES OF ENERGY

There are many different **types of energy** that exist. These include mechanical, sound, magnetic, electrical, light, heat, and chemical. From the first law of thermodynamics, we know that energy cannot be **created** or **destroyed**, but it may be **converted** from one form to another. This does not mean that all forms of energy are useful. Indeed, the second law states that net useful energy decreases in every process that takes place. Most often this occurs when other forms of energy are converted to heat through means such as friction. In these cases, the heat is quickly absorbed into the surroundings and becomes unusable.

ENERGY CONVERSION

There are many examples of energy conversion, such as in an automobile. The **chemical energy** in the gasoline is converted to **mechanical energy** in the engine. Subsequently, this mechanical energy is converted to **kinetic energy** as the car moves. Additionally, the mechanical energy is converted to **electrical energy** to power the radio, headlights, air conditioner, and other devices. In the radio, electrical energy is converted to **sound energy**. In the headlights, it is converted to **heat** and **light energy**. In the air conditioner, it does work to remove heat energy from the car's interior. It is important to remember that, in all of these processes, a portion of the energy is lost from its intended purpose.

EXAMPLES OF ENERGY

- Candles convert chemical energy to light and heat as they burn.
- Hydro-electric dams and wind turbines convert mechanical energy into electricity.
- The sun uses nuclear energy to create heat and light.
- Light bulbs convert electrical energy into light and heat.
- Speakers convert electricity into sound energy.

ELECTRICAL ENERGY AND CIRCUITS

Electrical energy is the energy of small particles called **electrons** moving from one material to another. All matter has electrons, but some materials allow for their electrons to move more freely, which is why some materials are conductive and others are not. Just like with magnets, electricity can have a positive, negative, or neutral charge. Also like with magnets, **opposite charges attract**, whereas same charges repel each other, which is why clothes that are charged with static electricity cling to each other. Lightning is another good example of an electrical charge in nature. Lightning is made by friction between the air and the ground, which causes the ground to become positively charged and the clouds become negatively charged. These charges want to balance out, so when the charges become strong enough, they snap back together suddenly, creating a lightning bolt and causing the charges to neutralize.

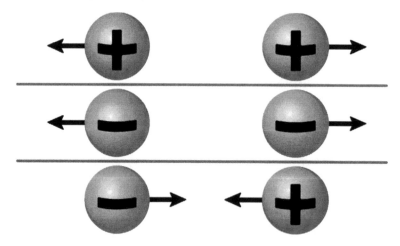

CIRCUITS

Electricity does not flow on its own; there needs to be both an imbalance of negative and positive charges and there needs to be a path for the electrons to **flow** through. This path is called a **circuit**, and it is made of a conductive material, such as wire, that completes a full circle. A circuit also needs to have a **power source**, such as a battery, that pushes the electrical imbalance. When a circuit is complete, electrical energy will flow from positive to negative. The flow of electricity through a circuit is called a **current**. Current can flow through other objects, such as a light bulb, to use energy without interrupting the circuit.

PARTS IN A CIRCUIT

One of the most common parts in a circuit is a switch. To work, a circuit must have a continuous path for the electrical energy to flow through. A switch is simply a device that physically cuts the circuit so that the energy cannot flow. When the circuit is cut, there is no path for the energy to flow. Other common parts in circuits allow the current to flow through them, converting the energy into other forms. These objects are called **load objects** or **resistors**, and they include light bulbs and motors. Light bulbs convert the electrical energy into light, while motors convert the electrical energy into mechanical energy.

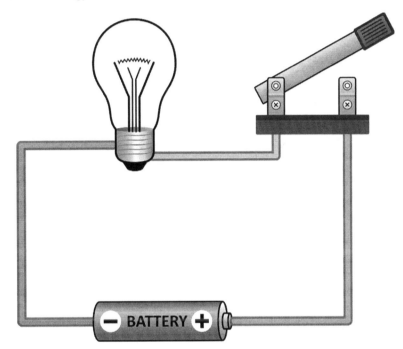

CONDUCTORS AND INSULATORS

The terms conductor and insulator refer to how easily a material transfers energy to and from another material. Usually, this refers to **thermal** and **electrical** energy. A **conductor** is a material that easily transfers the energy, whereas an **insulator** does not easily transfer energy. Most materials that conduct heat well also conduct electricity well, and vice-versa. One example of a good conductor is copper wire. Copper wire is used in many electrical applications because it conducts electricity well. Most metals, like copper, also conduct heat well and are used in cooking because they heat up quickly and transfer the energy to the food that is being cooked. Examples of insulators include plastic, wood, and air.

CONDUCTORS AND INSULATORS USED TOGETHER

Insulators and conductors are often used together for better effect. For instance, the handle on a frying pan is usually made of silicone or plastic because it does not conduct heat well, whereas the rest of the pan is metal, which does conduct heat. The insulating properties of the plastic handle protect the cook's hand from being burned, while the metal parts of the pan help to cook the food. Insulators are also often used alongside conductors in electrical parts to help direct the flow of electricity and protect from shocks and fires. For instance, most outlets have a mixture of plastic parts and metal parts. The cover and the box that holds the outlet in the wall are usually plastic, and

29

the wiring is covered with plastic to prevent shocks and fires, but the inside parts are usually made of copper, which help the electrical energy flow freely inside.

EXAMPLES OF CONDUCTORS AND INSULATORS

	Conductors	Insulators
Thermal	Aluminum, Copper, Silver, Diamonds	Plastic, Wood, Water, Air
Electrical	Gold, Steel, Copper, Water,	Rubber, Plastic, Glass, Rock, Wood, Air, Diamond

HEAT TRANSFER

Heat is a type of energy. Heat transfers from the hot object to the cold object through the three forms of heat transfer: conduction, convection, and radiation.

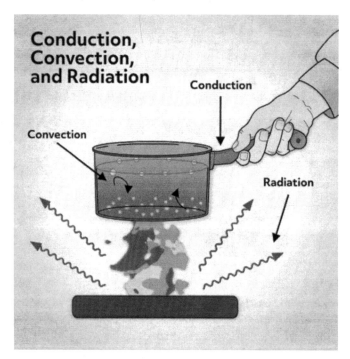

- **Conduction** is the transfer of heat by physical contact. When you touch a hot pot, the pot transfers heat to your hand by conduction.
- **Convection** is the transfer of heat by the movement of fluids. When you put your hand in steam, the steam transfers heat to your hand by convection.
- **Radiation** is the transfer of heat by electromagnetic waves. When you put your hand near a campfire, the fire heats your hand by radiation.

> **Review Video: Heat Transfer**
> Visit mometrix.com/academy and enter code: 451646

PROPERTIES OF LIGHT

Light is a type of energy that is technically on the electromagnetic spectrum. Other electromagnetic waves include x-rays and radio waves. They operate in the same way, but on a frequency that cannot be seen by the human eye. Light energy travels in a straight direction unless it touches another object and is interfered with. Therefore, if a flashlight were shined in space, it could be seen on the other side of the galaxy, so long as it did not run into an object.

REFLECTION

When light touches an object, it interacts in one of three ways. On shiny objects, such as mirrors, metal, and glass, at least some of the light energy **reflects**, causing it to suddenly change directions. The light's direction will be the opposite of its original angle.

REFRACTION

When light changes from one medium to another, the **frequency** of the light changes to match the new medium's **density**. Water is a different density than air, so when light enters water from the air, the angle of that light changes, which is called **refraction**. Because human vision is based on light, this produces an optical illusion when putting objects in water. If you were to insert a pencil into a cup of water, it would appear bent where the water starts.

ABSORPTION

Not all objects reflect well. When it touches an object that is not shiny, not much energy is reflected, but is instead **absorbed**. When light is absorbed, the type of energy is changed to **thermal energy**, causing a production of heat.

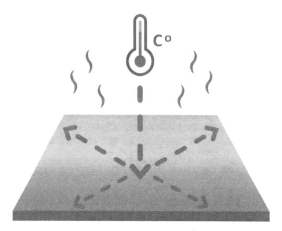

LIGHT AND DIFFERENT MEDIA

When talking about light, a medium is a substance that light travels through. In space, there is no air, so technically, there is no medium in space; this is called a vacuum. On Earth, light travels through air or water as its medium. Even though air is invisible, it still interferes with light slightly, causing it to diffract, or spread out. That is why a flashlight does not shine a perfectly straight line of light, but it spreads out and gets weaker with distance from the light source.

GRAVITY

Gravity is a force that exists between all objects with matter. **Gravity** is a pulling force between objects, meaning that the forces on the objects point toward the opposite object. Gravity as we experience it is the force that the Earth exerts on objects, pulling them downward toward the center of the Earth. When Newton's third law is applied to gravity, the force pairs from gravity are shown to be equal in magnitude and opposite in direction.

Technically, all matter pulls other matter. The more massive the object, the more it pulls. The Earth is seen as our center of gravity because it is the most massive object nearby. Gravity is also reason that the Earth and other planets revolve around the Sun. The Sun is so massive that the Earth and all of the other bodies within the solar system are drawn to it and revolve around it as a result.

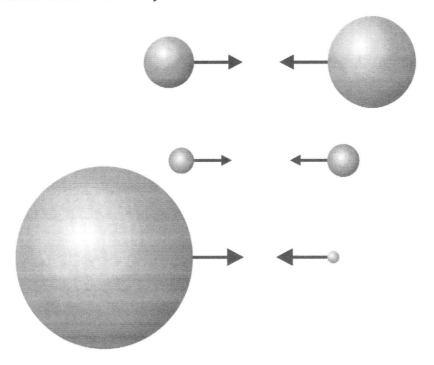

FRICTION

Friction is a resistance to motion between contacting surfaces. In order to illustrate the concept of friction, let us imagine a book resting on a table. As it sits, the force of its weight is equal to and opposite of the normal force. If, however, we were to exert a force on the book, attempting to push it to one side, a frictional force would arise, equal and opposite to our force. This kind of frictional force is known as static frictional force.

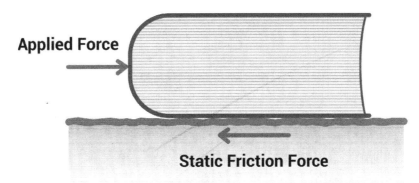

33

As we increase our force on the book, however, we will eventually cause it to accelerate in the direction of our force. At this point, the frictional force opposing us will be known as kinetic friction. For many combinations of surfaces, the magnitude of the kinetic frictional force is lower than that of the static frictional force, and consequently, the amount of force needed to maintain the movement of the book will be less than that needed to initiate the movement.

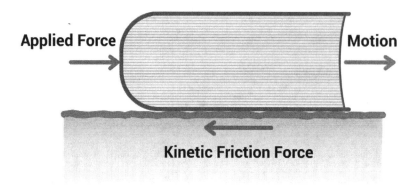

MAGNETISM

Magnetism is an **attraction** between opposite poles of **magnetic materials** and a **repulsion** between similar poles of magnetic materials. Magnetism can be natural or induced with the use of electric currents. Magnets almost always exist with two polar sides: north and south. A magnetic force exists between two poles on objects. Different poles attract each other. Like poles repel each other.

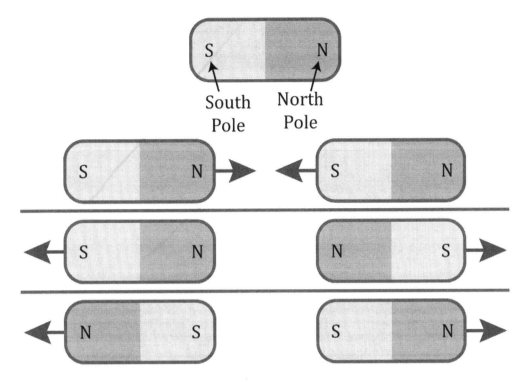

South Pole   North Pole

MOTION AND FORCE

Sir Isaac Newton observed three major laws explaining how the motion of an object works. The term **motion** refers to the movement of an object and the term **force** refers to physical energy that is applied to an object. Newton also referred to objects that are not moving as being in a state of **rest**.

- **Newton's First Law of Motion** - a body will remain at **rest** or in **motion** until a **force** is applied to it.
  - A bowling ball continues to roll in the same direction it was thrown until friction eventually slows it down.
  - A ball sitting on the ground will not move unless a force is applied to it.

- **Newton's Second Law of Motion** -the amount of **acceleration** is determined by the amount of **force** and the **mass** of the object being moved.
  - o A soccer ball will accelerate more if kicked harder.

  - o A shopping cart is much easier to push than a car because it is much less massive.

- **Newton's Third Law of Motion** – For every **action**, there is an equal and opposite **reaction**.
  - o The floor applies force upward to hold up the weight of a person standing on it.
  - o A dog pulls against a leash that his owner is holding.

DIRECTIONS OF MOTION

Motion can be either linear, rotational, or oscillating.

- **Linear motion** - a single direction, like a bowling ball rolling down the lane or a train moving in one direction down its tracks.
- **Rotational motion** – rotating or spinning in a circular motion, such as a top spinning, a merry-go-round, or the Earth rotating around the Sun.
- **Oscillating motion** – bouncing up and down repeatedly, such as a yo-yo on a string or a spring. This also includes waves as they rise and fall.

MECHANICAL ADVANTAGE

Simple machines include the inclined plane, lever, wheel and axle, and pulley. These simple machines have no internal source of energy. More complex or compound machines can be formed from them. Simple machines provide a force known as a mechanical advantage and make it easier to accomplish a task. The inclined plane enables a force less than the object's weight to be used to push an object to a greater height. A lever enables a multiplication of force. The wheel and axle allows for movement with less resistance. Single or double pulleys allow for easier direction of force. The wedge and screw are forms of the inclined plane. A wedge turns a smaller force working over a greater distance into a larger force. The screw is similar to an incline that is wrapped around a shaft.

INCLINED PLANES

An **inclined plane** is a flat surface with one end raised higher than the other— like a ramp. It works similar to a lever. By pushing a heavy object over a longer distance (the inclined plane), the object can be raised a shorter distance in height with a smaller force than it would take to lift it straight up. The longer the inclined plane, the less force is required to raise the object. This is also a simple machine.

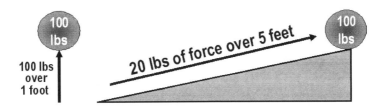

LEVERS

A **lever** is a simple machine made up of a rigid rod or beam that rotates on a fixed pivot or **fulcrum**. It can be used to lift a heavy mass by applying a small force over a large distance at one end to exert a much larger force over a shorter distance at the other end. Seesaws, crowbars, and shovels are all levers. Increasing the length of the lever arm decreases the necessary force required to lift the weight. A lever is a simple machine.

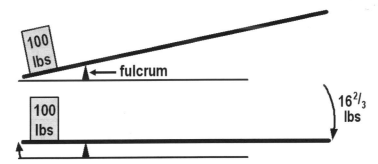

SCREWS

A screw is another kind of simple machine. It turns rotational force (the turning of the screw) into forward or linear force that makes the screw bore into wood or other substance. The screw is an inclined plane wrapped around a central nail. The force of turning the screw with a screwdriver acts along the longer distance of the spiral inclined plane to penetrate a shorter distance into the wood. It takes less force to turn the screw than to hammer a nail into the wood.

WEDGES

Still another kind of simple machine is a wedge, like an axe or a knife. A wedge concentrates and converts a downward force into a sideways force. It cuts down into an object and pushes the sections to the side. A nail is also a wedge.

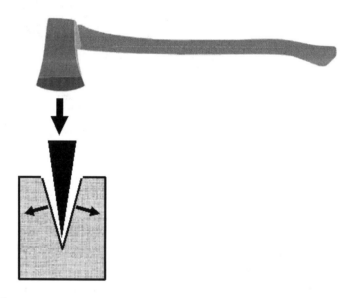

WHEELS AND AXLES

A wheel and axle is a type of simple machine. A wheel is basically a large circular lever attached to a much smaller axle. By applying a small force to turn the wheel a longer distance around the wheel, a much larger force is given to the smaller diameter axle. A doorknob is an example. The wider the knob the easier it is to open the door latch.

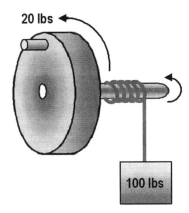

PULLEYS

A pulley is one or more wheels with grooved rims through which a rope or cable runs to change the direction of pull and lift a load. With just a single fixed pulley the amount of force needed to lift a weight is the same as the weight. But if a second moveable pulley is added as shown here, the amount of force needed to lift the weight is cut in half — just 50 pounds.

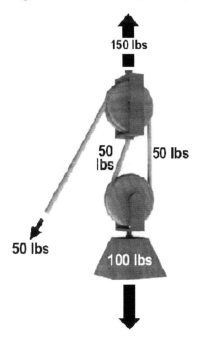

LIQUID WATER VS. ICE

There is a difference in state. The water in the glass is a liquid, while that in the pail is a solid. The liquid water flows and takes the shape of its container. The solid ice does not flow and does not assume the shape of the pail. The ice is also less dense than the water and will float in the water.

COMPLEX MACHINES

A complex machine is a machine that combines two or more simple machines. For example a pair of scissors is made up of two wedges acting in opposite directions connected by a lever.

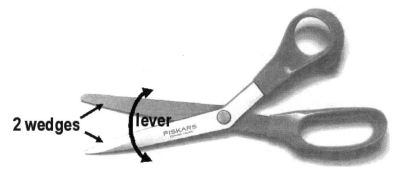

WHEELBARROWS

A wheelbarrow is a complex machine. It is a lever mounted on a wheel and axle.

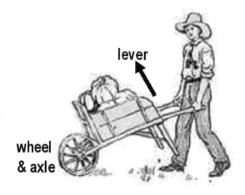

SAW

A saw is actually a complex machine. Each tooth in a saw blade is a wedge. Therefore, a saw consists of many wedges, which makes it a complex machine. When a person saws a piece of wood, he exerts both a downward force and a back and forth force. This cuts into the wood and pushes the two sides apart just like an axe.

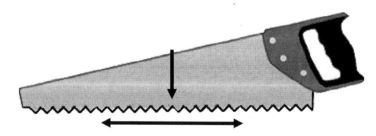

Earth and Space Science

ROCK CYCLE

The **rock cycle** is the process whereby the materials that make up the Earth transition through the three types of rock: igneous, sedimentary, and metamorphic. Rocks, like all matter, cannot be created or destroyed; rather, they undergo a series of changes and adopt different forms through the functions of the rock cycle. Plate tectonics and the water cycle are the driving forces behind the rock cycle; they force rocks and minerals out of equilibrium and force them to adjust to different external conditions. Viewed in a generalized, cyclical fashion, the rock cycle operates as follows: rocks beneath Earth's surface melt into magma. This **magma** either erupts through volcanoes or remains inside the Earth. Regardless, the magma cools, forming igneous rocks. On the surface, these rocks experience **weathering** and **erosion**, which break them down and distribute the fragments across the surface. These fragments form layers and eventually become **sedimentary rocks**. Sedimentary rocks are then either transformed to **metamorphic rocks** (which will become magma inside the Earth) or melted down into magma.

ROCK FORMATION

Igneous Rocks: Igneous rocks can be formed from sedimentary rocks, metamorphic rocks, or other igneous rocks. Rocks that are pushed under the Earth's surface (usually due to plate subduction) are exposed to high mantle temperatures, which cause the rocks to melt into magma. The magma then rises to the surface through volcanic processes. The lower atmospheric temperature causes the magma to cool, forming grainy, extrusive igneous rocks. The creation of extrusive, or volcanic, rocks is quite rapid. The cooling process can occur so rapidly that crystals do not form; in this case, the result is a glass, such as obsidian. It is also possible for magma to cool down inside the Earth's interior; this type of igneous rock is called intrusive. Intrusive, or plutonic, rocks cool more slowly, resulting in a coarse-grained texture.

Sedimentary Rocks: Sedimentary rocks are formed when rocks at the Earth's surface experience weathering and erosion, which break them down and distribute the fragments across the surface. Fragmented material (small pieces of rock, organic debris, and the chemical products of mineral sublimation) is deposited and accumulates in layers, with top layers burying the materials beneath. The pressure exerted by the topmost layers causes the lower layers to compact, creating solid sedimentary rock in a process called lithification.

Metamorphic Rocks: Metamorphic rocks are igneous or sedimentary rocks that have "morphed" into another kind of rock. In metamorphism, high temperatures and levels of pressure change preexisting rocks physically and/or chemically, which produces different species of rocks. In the rock cycle, this process generally occurs in materials that have been thrust back into the Earth's mantle by plate subduction. Regional metamorphism refers to a large band of metamorphic activity; this often occurs near areas of high orogenic (mountain-building) activity. Contact metamorphism refers to metamorphism that occurs when "country rock" (that is, rock native to an area) comes into contact with high-heat igneous intrusions (magma).

FORMATION OF DELTAS, CANYONS, AND DUNES

A **delta** is landform that is created at the mouth of a river, where it flows into a larger body of water. The river carries sediment and when it reaches the larger body of water it spreads out and deposits the sediment. An example would be the Mississippi Delta, where the Mississippi River meets the Gulf of Mexico. A **canyon** is a deep ravine between two cliffs. It is usually formed by the erosion of flowing water over extended periods of time. A famous example of this is the Grand Canyon in Arizona. A **sand dune** is a mound of sand built by natural forces, usually wind, over time.

Great Sand Dunes National Park, located in Colorado, is home to the tallest sand dunes in the United States.

ROLE OF WATER

Water plays an important role in the rock cycle through its roles in **erosion** and **weathering**: it wears down rocks; it contributes to the dissolution of rocks and minerals as acidic soil water; and it carries ions and rock fragments (sediments) to basins where they will be compressed into **sedimentary rock**. Water also plays a role in the **metamorphic processes** that occur underwater in newly-formed igneous rock at mid-ocean ridges. The presence of water (and other volatiles) is a vital component in the melting of rocky crust into magma above subduction zones.

> **Review Video: Igneous, Sedimentary, and Metamorphic Rocks**
> Visit mometrix.com/academy and enter code: 689294

SOILS

Soils are formed when rock is broken down into smaller and smaller fragments by physical, chemical, and biological processes. This is called **weathering**. *Physical processes* include **erosion** and **transportation** by water and wind, freezing and thawing, and slumping due to gravity. *Chemical changes* alter the original substances present in rocks and early-stage soils. *Biological processes* include burrowing by animals like earthworms and rodents and penetration by plant roots. As plants and animals die and **decay**, soils become rich in dark organic matter called *humus*.

PROPERTIES OF SOIL

Since soil is a mixture of rock fragments and biological materials, it varies significantly. The composition of soil determines whether it will be good for plant life or not. Several properties of soil can be used to identify its composition, which can be helpful for adjusting it for suitability for plant growth.

- **Texture** refers to the size of the particles, which are classified as sand, silt, or clay, depending on the size and mixture of the particles.
- **Structure** refers to the density and arrangement of the soil particles. Soil can be compacted, making it dense and rock-like or it can be loose and easy to work with when planting.
- **Porosity** refers to how well water flows through the soil. A higher sand content usually allows water to flow through the soil more easily, whereas clay tends to hold onto water.
- **Chemistry** cannot be seen, but can be tested for the actual elements present in a sample of soil.
- **Color** of soil changes based on the types of minerals and organic matter in the soil. Redder soil may indicate that there is oxidized (rusted) iron in the soil, for instance.

42

NATURAL RESOURCES

The term **natural resources** refers to products and energy that can be harvested from the world and used.

- **Water** is one of the most abundant resources on the earth and is necessary for life.
- **Natural gas** and **oil** exist underground and deep in the ocean and can be used as fuel for machines.
- **Trees** can be harvested for wood and paper and other byproducts that are used in daily life.
- **Metals** can be harvested from the ground and are used in many applications, such as building materials and in electronics.
- **Sand** can be used to make glass, soaps, and electronics.
- **Sunlight** and **wind** can be harvested with solar panels and wind turbines to generate electricity.
- **Animal products** are used for food or materials in clothing and some manufacturing processes.

RENEWABLE AND NON-RENEWABLE RESOURCES

Materials and energy on the Earth are classified as either renewable or non-renewable. The term **renewable resources** refers to resources that are not going to run out due to overuse or can be easily reclaimed once used. This includes the sun, wind, and water. Some plants and animals grow so fast that it would be very challenging to run out and cause any form of extinction. **Non-renewable resources** include materials that take a very long time to produce, such as fossil fuels and coal. Once the Earth's population uses these materials up, it is very difficult to obtain or impossible to create more. Because renewable resources do not run out, whereas non-renewable resources do, environmentalists and scientists are always looking for new renewable resources to supply the planet with energy and for ways to reduce consumption of non-renewable resources. This reduction of consumption is known as **conservation**.

WEATHER

Heat energy from the sun warms different parts of the planet in different ways at different times. As warm air rises it expands and cools. This causes moisture to condense as liquid drops or freeze as ice crystals to form clouds. When the water drops or ice crystals become too large to stay aloft, they fall as precipitation. As warm air rises it also leaves a low pressure zone behind. This causes air from high surrounding high pressure zones to rush in as wind.

CLOUDS

Clouds form when water vapor in the atmosphere cools to the point where it condenses out as water droplets or small particles of frozen ice crystals that we can see. Clouds can also form when more moisture is added to the air by evaporation until the air becomes saturated and cannot hold any more water. Then the water vapor will begin to condense into visible droplets.

PRECIPITATION FALLING FROM A CLOUD

When the condensed water droplets or ice crystals forming in the cloud grow in size and become too heavy to stay aloft, they fall as rain, snowflakes, or hail.

LIGHTNING BOLT

Lightning is a huge electric spark that can occur inside a cloud, go from one cloud to another, or go from a cloud to the ground. The turbulent rising air and rising and falling raindrops or ice crystals in a thunderstorm cause differences in electric charge in different parts of the cloud and between the bottom of the cloud and the ground. When the difference in charge is large enough, a lightning bolt will discharge which neutralizes the difference.

THUNDER

As a lightning bolt travels through the air, it pushes the air aside faster than the speed of sound. This produces a shock wave of very hot air that creates a loud sonic boom, which we hear as thunder. If a person can hear thunder, he needs to get indoors quickly as possible since he could be struck by lightning.

We hear thunder later because sound travels much slower than light. Light travels so fast that it is almost instantaneous from one point to another anywhere on Earth. Sound travels much more slowly—about one mile every five seconds or so. Light would travel one mile in only about 5 millionths of a second. Therefore, the distance from a lightning flash can be determined by counting the number of seconds until the thunder it made is heard.

TORNADO

A tornado is a violent rotating column of air that is in contact with both the ground and a cloud. The column is visible because the very low pressure causes water vapor to condense out as visible water droplets. Where the tornado touches the ground it usually stirs up a cloud of dirt and debris like the one in this photo. Tornadoes are the most violent storms on Earth, and the strongest spin at 300 miles per hour.

HURRICANE

A **hurricane** is a very large tropical storm that forms over the open ocean and produces very strong winds and heavy rains. A **tropical storm** forms when warm water evaporates and the saturated air

44

rises and forms a column of condensed water vapor. As the wind speed increases the pressure falls even more and a hurricane can be born. Sinking air in the center of the storm produces an **eye** (arrow) where the weather is quite calm and free of clouds.

MEASURING WEATHER

Weather can be measured by a variety of methods. The simplest include measurement of rainfall, sunshine, pressure, humidity, temperature, and cloudiness with basic instruments such as thermometers, barometers, and rain gauges. However, the use of **radar** (which involves analysis of microwaves reflecting off of raindrops) and satellite imagery grants meteorologists a look at the big picture of weather across, for example, an entire continent. This helps them understand and make predictions about current and developing weather systems. Infrared (heat-sensing) imaging allows meteorologists to measure the temperature of clouds above ground. Using weather reports gathered from different weather stations spread over an area, meteorologists create synoptic charts. The locations and weather reports of several stations are plotted on a chart; analysis of the pressures reported from each location, as well as rainfall, cloud cover, and so on, can reveal basic weather patterns.

WATER CYCLE

The **water cycle** refers to the circulation of water in the Earth's hydrosphere (below the surface, on the surface, and above the surface of the Earth). This continuous process involves five physical actions.

- **Evaporation** refers to liquid water heating up and changing to into a gas, known as water vapor.
- **Transpiration** is where water inside of plants evaporates directly out of plant leaves.
- **Condensation** refers to the water vapor cooling down and beginning to turn back into a liquid form, causing clouds to form.
- **Precipitation** refers to the rain, snow, hail, or sleet that falls from clouds once the water vapor has condensed enough.

- The **storage** stage of the water cycle refers to the water being stored in the ground, trees, or bodies of water on the earth. Water is either trapped in vegetation (interception) or absorbed into the surface (infiltration). Runoff, caused by gravity, physically moves water downward into oceans or other water bodies.

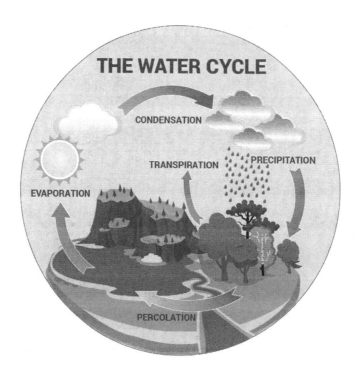

Review Video: Hydrologic Cycle
Visit mometrix.com/academy and enter code: 426578

SUN

The **Sun** is the vital force of life on Earth; it is also the central component of our solar system. It is basically a sphere of extremely hot gases (close to 15 million degrees at the core) held together by gravity. Some of these gaseous molecules are ionized due to the high temperatures. The balance between its gravitational force and the pressure produced by the hot gases is called **hydrostatic equilibrium**. The source of the solar energy that keeps the Sun alive and plays a key role in the perpetuation of life on Earth is located in the Sun's core, where nucleosynthesis produces heat energy and photons. The Sun's atmosphere consists of the photosphere, the surface visible from Earth, the chromosphere, a layer outside of and hotter than the photosphere, the transition zone (the region where temperatures rise between the chromosphere and the corona), and the corona, which is best viewed at x-ray wavelengths. A solar flare is an explosive emission of ionized particles from the Sun's surface.

Review Video: The Sun
Visit mometrix.com/academy and enter code: 699233

EARTH'S ROTATION

The **Earth rotates** west to east about its axis, an imaginary straight line that runs nearly vertically through the center of the planet. This rotation (which takes 23 hours, 56 minutes, and 5 seconds) places each section of the Earth's surface in a position facing the Sun for a period of time, thus creating the alternating periods of light and darkness we experience as **day and night**. This rotation constitutes a sidereal day; it is measured as the amount of time required for a reference star to cross the meridian (an imaginary north-south line above an observer). Each star crosses the meridian once every (sidereal) day. Since the speed at which Earth rotates is not exactly constant, we use the mean solar day (a 24-hour period) in timekeeping rather than the slightly variable sidereal day.

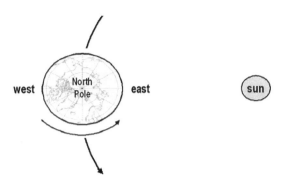

EARTH'S REVOLUTION AROUND THE SUN

Like all celestial objects in our solar system, planet **Earth** revolves around the **Sun**. This process takes approximately 365 1/4 days, the period of time that constitutes a calendar year. The path of the orbit of Earth around the Sun is not circular but **elliptical**. Therefore, the distances between the Earth and the Sun at points on either extreme of this counterclockwise orbit are not equal. In other words, the distance between the two objects varies over the course of a year. At **perihelion**, the minimum heliocentric distance, Earth is 147 million kilometers from the Sun. At **aphelion**, the maximum heliocentric distance, Earth is 152 million kilometers from the Sun. This movement of the Earth is responsible for the apparent annual motions of the Sun (in a path referred to as the ecliptic) and other celestial objects visible from Earth's surface.

> **Review Video: Astronomy**
> Visit mometrix.com/academy and enter code: 640556
>
> **Review Video: Solar System**
> Visit mometrix.com/academy and enter code: 273231

PHASES OF THE MOON

As the moon revolves around Earth approximately every 27.3 days, light from the Sun hits it from different angles. This causes the Moon to be in full sunlight (full moon) when Earth is between it and the Sun, complete darkness (new moon) when it is between Earth and the Sun, and all stages in between. When the Moon is half in sunlight and half in shadow it is in the first or last quarter, depending on whether it is heading towards becoming a full moon or a new moon.

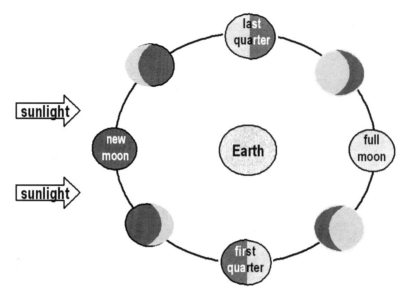

EARTH'S ATMOSPHERE

Earth's gravity is strong enough to attract the molecules of the gases in the atmosphere and keep them in a layer surrounding the planet. The gravity of smaller celestial bodies like Mercury and Earth's moon is not strong enough to do this, and their atmospheres long ago diffused out into space.

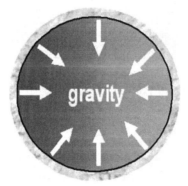

SEASONS

Earth is tilted on its axis as it revolves around the Sun and rotates upon its axis from left to right. That means more sunshine and longer days and shorter nights in the hemisphere facing the Sun. More sunlight means warmer temperatures. In the left-hand picture the Southern Hemisphere is experiencing its summer. Six months later when Earth is on the opposite side of the Sun it is the Northern Hemisphere that is having summer.

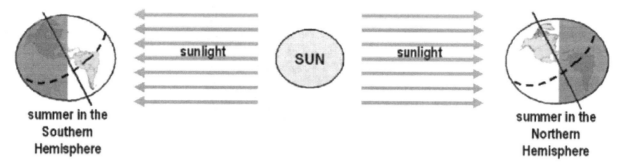

summer in the Southern Hemisphere

summer in the Northern Hemisphere

SOLAR SYSTEM

The *solar system* consists of the sun and eight *major planets*. In order from the sun the planets are Mercury, Venus, Earth, Mars, Jupiter, Saturn, Uranus and Neptune. Pluto is no longer considered to be a major planet. Along with 5 other similar sized objects it is now a *minor planet*. Six of the major planets have one or more moons. The solar system also contains countless *meteoroids*, *asteroids*, and *comets*.

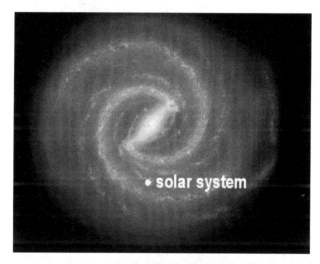

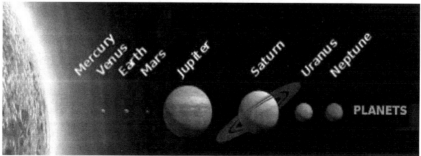

MILKY WAY

On a clear dark moonless night far from city lights a broad white band of stars that stretches across the sky can be seen. This is the Milky Way galaxy, and our sun and the solar system are part of it.

The Milky Way is a huge flat disk containing between 200 billion and 400 billion stars. Because Earth is in that disk, we see it edge on, which is why it appears to us as a broad band of light.

The Milky Way is a flat, disk-shaped spiral galaxy with a central bar-like bulge of stars. It is huge—between 100,000 and 120,000 light-years in diameter. A light-year is a unit of distance, not time. It is the distance light travels in one year, about 6 trillion miles. The Milky Way is between 600 thousand trillion and 700 thousand trillion miles across. Our solar system lies about two thirds of the way out on one of the spiral arms.

COMET

Comets are small icy bodies ranging in size from tens of yards to tens of miles in diameter. They orbit the sun with periods of a few years to hundreds of thousands of years. Halley's comet shown here orbits the sun every 75 to 76 years. As a comet nears the sun a long tail or coma is created as ice and dust are blown off by the intense radiation and the solar wind of charged particles from the sun.

METEOROIDS AND METEORS

A *meteoroid* is a sand- to boulder-sized piece of debris hurtling through the solar system at speeds of between 15 and 45 miles per second. When it enters earth's atmosphere it burns up and leaves a visible fiery trail of gas and debris called a *meteor*. Some meteoroids are large enough that they do not completely burn up, and what remains reaches the ground. These are called *meteorites*. Meteoroids can be small pieces that have broken off of *asteroids*.

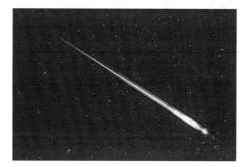

Organisms and Environments

PRODUCERS, CONSUMERS, AND DECOMPOSERS

Producers are organisms that can make their own food. Most producers are plants. Through photosynthesis plants make sugars that provide energy. Plants only need sunlight, water, and the proper minerals and other nutrients to live, grow, and reproduce themselves. **Consumers** are organisms that eat other organisms. Consumers are animals that eat plants or other animals that eat plants. Decomposers are organisms that feed on decaying plant and animal matter. Since decomposers cannot make their own food they are classified as consumers. Fungi such as mushrooms are **decomposers** that break down the tissues and wood of living or dead plants or the bodies of dead animals.

ENERGY PYRAMID

Energy flow through an ecosystem can be tracked through an energy pyramid. An **energy pyramid** shows how energy is transferred from one trophic level to another. **Producers** always form the base of an energy pyramid, and the consumers form successive levels above the producers. Producers only store about 1% of the solar energy they receive. Then, each successive level only uses about 10% of the energy of the previous level. That means that **primary consumers** use about 10% of the energy used by primary producers, such as grasses and trees. Next, **secondary consumers** use 10% of primary consumers' 10%, or 1% overall. This continues up for as many trophic levels as exist in a particular ecosystem.

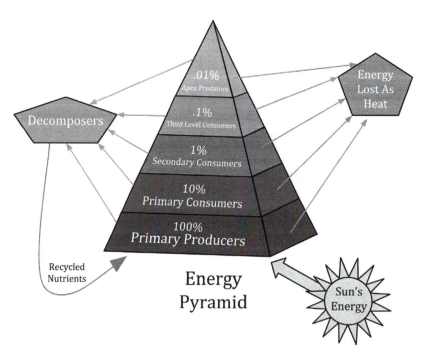

FOOD WEB

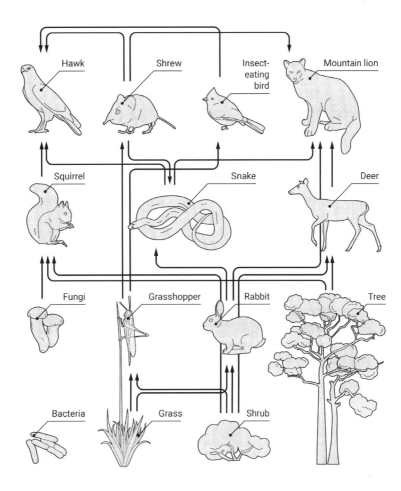

Energy flow through an ecosystem can be illustrated by a **food web**. Energy moves through the food web in the direction of the arrows. In the food web, **producers** such as grass, trees, and shrubs use energy from the sun to produce food through photosynthesis. **Herbivores** or **primary consumers** such as squirrels, grasshoppers, and rabbits obtain energy by eating the producers. **Secondary consumers**, which are carnivores such as snakes and shrews, obtain energy by eating the primary consumers. **Tertiary consumers**, which are carnivores such as hawks and mountain lions, obtain energy by eating the secondary consumers.

> **Review Video: Food Webs**
> Visit mometrix.com/academy and enter code: 853254

INTERDEPENDENCE OF THE FOOD WEB

Because each level of consumer is dependent on the previous level for food, the population of each level affects the other animal groups. For instance, if an ecosystem is made up of only grass, deer, and wolves, the grass are the producers, the deer eat the grass, and the wolves eat the deer. If deer are overhunted one year, the grass is given room to grow more because less of it is consumed, but the wolves will not have enough food, so the population will reduce size. Eventually, because of the abundance of grass and a reduced population of wolves, the deer may then have a surge of population. This example is an over-simplistic example, as there are usually many more producers, consumers, and predators within an ecosystem.

POPULATIONS OF ANIMALS OR PLANTS

A population consists of all of the organisms of a certain kind in a defined area, region, or habitat. It may be all the red foxes in a given national park, all the loblolly pines in Virginia (very hard to count), all the bullfrogs in a certain pond, or even all of the boxelder bugs on a single box elder tree. In the case of rare or endangered species it may be all of the individuals still living in the wild.

Several factors operate to keep animal and plant populations under control. Predation, grazing, disease, competition for limiting resources such as food or nutrients, water, habitat and living space, hunting and breeding territory, and sunlight for plants all play important roles. Even the size of the population can influence factors such as birth rate and severity of disease outbreaks or force individuals to migrate to other less crowded areas.

PLANT SPECIES COMPETING WITH EACH OTHER

Creosote bush is the most widespread shrub in the deserts of the American Southwest where water can be very scarce for long periods. The roots of mature creosote bushes are extremely efficient and absorb all the water in the sandy soil around them. This creates very dry zones around each plant. The seeds of other plants cannot survive long enough to germinate. Therefore, the plants tend to be spaced far apart from each other.

FOOD WEB IN A POND

Sunlight allows green algae to photosynthesize and grow. The algae are fed upon by small animals like water fleas and copepods. In turn, these are eaten by small worms, mosquito larvae and other larval insects. These are then eaten by mosquito fish, which in turn are eaten by larger fishes like bluegills. The bluegills are preyed upon by even larger fishes like bass and by herons, egrets and raccoons (which also eat the bass). Then the animal waste and everything that dies and settles to the bottom is decomposed by bacteria and fungi.

FOOD WEB IN A MEADOW

Sunlight allows grass and other plants to grow. These plants are eaten by a variety of *herbivores* like insects, rodents, and rabbits. Their seeds are consumed by various birds such as sparrows and quail. The insects are eaten by *carnivores*, including other kinds of birds, shrews, and bats. The rodents, rabbits, and some of the birds are then eaten by larger carnivores like weasels and foxes. Also, the quail, mice, rabbits and shrews are eaten by owls at night and by hawks during the day.

ANIMALS OF THE SAME SPECIES COMPETING WITH EACH OTHER

Male elk known as bulls have large antlers, which they shed and regrow each year. Like their smaller deer cousins, bull elk engage in bugling contests and ritual combat (like the photo below) to dominate other males and win all the female (cow) elk in a harem.

Different species of animals often compete for food. The spotted hyena and the African lion shown here compete for prey like zebras and wildebeest. Both hyenas and lions run in groups. A larger pack of hyenas can drive a smaller pride of lions away from prey the lions have killed. However, one lion can easily kill one or more hyenas. They rarely tolerate each other as they seem to be doing below.

ANIMAL MIGRATION

Many animals make a regular two-way, long-distance journey due to seasonal changes affecting the availability of food, weather or rainfall. Birds are especially noted for this, but other animals like bats, some butterflies, moths, and grasshoppers also migrate back and forth between northern winter and southern summer territories. Caribou and wildebeest also make spectacular migrations. The figure at right shows the 14,000-mile migration route of the Swainson's hawk, which spends its summers in western North America and winters in South America.

LEARNED BEHAVIORS IN ANIMALS

Many behaviors in higher animals such as birds and mammals actually have to be learned. Bird songs are usually learned. Male cardinals sing slightly different songs in different areas of the country. They learn these dialects from the adult birds around them. Also, unlike the instinctive migration of spawning salmon, sandhill cranes must be taught the long migration routes they fly between their nesting and winter grounds. Likewise, most predatory mammals must learn how to hunt from their mothers.

FASTEST LAND ANIMAL

The fastest animal on planet Earth is the cheetah. A cheetah can run between 70 and 75 miles per hour for almost two thirds of a mile and can go from a dead stop to 62 miles per hour in three seconds. It stalks its small antelope prey to within a short distance and then chases it down. Since the gazelle being chased in this picture can only run at 50 miles per hour, the faster cheetah has a good chance of running it down.

ANIMALS THAT MOSTLY COME OUT AT NIGHT

Nocturnal animals are active at night and sleep during the day. Nocturnal animals generally have very good senses of hearing and smell, and specially adapted eyes for seeing in the dark. Hunting or foraging for food at night is one way of avoiding competition for those resources from *diurnal* animals that are active during the day. Hawks and owls avoid competing with each other for prey in this way. Nocturnal animals also avoid the intense heat of the day in hot regions like deserts.

HIBERNATION

Hibernation occurs when an animal enters a state of inactivity in which its body temperature drops, and its breathing and metabolism slow down, and it goes into a deep sleep for many days, weeks, or even months. This allows animals to survive long, cold winters when food is scarce. Bears, ground squirrels and other rodents, some bats like the one shown hibernating here, and certain kinds of snakes are known to hibernate. Some animals sleep through hot summer weather or droughts. This is called *aestivation*.

ORGANISMS AND ADAPTED ENVIRONMENT

Animals and plants are adapted to live in their environments in many special ways. For example, polar bears have white fur as camouflage which helps them blend in with their icy and snowy background. This makes it easier to sneak up on the seals on which they prey. They also have thick fur and a thick layer of blubber to help keep them warm in their frigid environment.

INSTINCTIVE BEHAVIORS

Instinctive behaviors are actions that are automatic in an animal and do not have to be taught or learned. Newly hatched sea turtles automatically crawl across the beach towards the ocean with no mother around to show them what to do. Tree squirrels automatically store acorns and nuts during the summer in order to have food in the coming winter. Also, salmon automatically return from the ocean to the freshwater river where they hatched in order to spawn.

CAMOUFLAGE AND MIMICRY

Generally speaking, *camouflage* is when an organism blends in with its surroundings in a way that it cannot be seen as in the case of the flounder blending in with the gravel on the bottom of a lake (Fig. B). *Mimicry* is when an organism resembles something else, like the leaf insect in Fig. A. In these two examples each animal is able to avoid being seen and eaten by a predator. However, sometimes it is the predator that is camouflaged or a mimic which enables it to pounce on its unsuspecting prey.

WARNING COLORATION

Dangerously venomous or poisonous animals often are brightly colored to warn predators that they are best left alone. This is called aposematic coloration. The deadly venomous coral snake (Fig. A.)

has bright red, yellow and black bands that circle its body. The harmless milk snake (Fig. B) mimics the dangerous coral snake which fools predators to leave them alone, too.

COMPETITION BETWEEN DIFFERENT ORGANISMS

Animals and plants have to compete with other species for food or nutrients, water, a place to live, nesting or breeding sites, sunlight in the case of plants, and other factors in the environment that may be scarce or limiting. Also, animals and plants of the same species have to compete with each other for the same things, as well in some cases for the right to breed and reproduce.

GENETICS AND HEREDITY

Genetics is the study of biological inheritance in organisms. Animals generally reproduce with a mother and a father, which both contribute their **genetic** information to offspring. The passing along of genetic traits is also known as **heredity**. The offspring of a mother with red hair and blue eyes with a father who has brown hair and brown eyes may receive any combination of those traits. Another example may be a red fox mating with a brown fox; the offspring may have either brown fur or red fur, and a pack of siblings may have a mixture of inherited traits. This type of inheritance can also be seen in plant life, as pink and white flowered plants may breed together to produce either pink or white flowered offspring, or even special hybrids with blended colors.

INNATE BEHAVIORS

Similar to genetics, there are some behaviors that are innate, or instinctual. Many animals do not nurture their young, but instead, the newborn creatures are capable of fending for themselves. Below are some examples of innate behaviors that are not learned or taught.

- Birds migrate from North to South for the winter to protect themselves from the cold.
- Salmon swim upstream to nesting grounds.
- Some insects migrate and form cocoons to metamorphose.
- Rattlesnakes shake their rattles to warn other animals.

LEARNED BEHAVIORS

Some behaviors and traits may be inherited, but many behaviors must be taught by the parents or pack to the young. Below are some examples of learned or taught behaviors.

- A wolf pack teaches the young wolves how to hunt effectively as a group.
- Some primates use sticks as tools to gather food.
- Dogs learn tricks and commands from their owners.
- Pelicans learn to hunt for fish in groups.
- Humans teach their children words and how to read.

CHANGES THROUGHOUT THE LIFE CYCLE

Many types of plants and animals go through a process of changes throughout their lifespan. This process involves a complete change in how the plant or animal looks and acts during that life stage. In insects and in amphibians, this is called **metamorphosis**.

TOMATO PLANT LIFE CYCLE

Tomato plants undergo a series of life stages, starting at the seed. The **seed** contains all of its own nutrition for the beginning stages of life. Once it is planted, it grows into a **seedling** and starts using photosynthesis to harness the energy for life and growth. When the plant is **mature**, it produces **flowers** which then produce the tomato fruit. The **fruit** contains seeds which then go on to become the next generation for this plant. The tomato plant usually dies after one year, so the next generation comes directly from the seeds of the previous generation.

LIMA BEAN LIFE CYCLE

Lima beans have similar life cycles are similar to that of a tomato plan. It begins are a seed, which grows roots underground. As it grows and emerges from the soil, it becomes a seedling, which eventually becomes an adult lima bean plant. Rather than flowering, it produces leaves and pods, which contain several new seeds. These seeds are known as beans, which can be replanted or cooked for food.

RADISH LIFE CYCLE

Radishes also begin as a seed, which germinates into a sprout. The radish grows large leaves above ground while the root underground also grows large and round. When the plant grows into an adult, it flowers, producing more seeds. The large root underground is generally what most people think of as a radish, and the leaves that grow above ground are known as radish greens. Both the root and the leaves are cooked and eaten.

FROG LIFE CYCLE

Frogs have a very distinctive life cycle. Frogs start out as eggs, which hatch into tadpoles. Tadpoles live and breathe completely in the water using gills and have no legs or arms to walk with. As the tadpole begins to mature, it grows legs and eventually becomes a young frog. The young frogs then emerge from the water and usually live on land and breathe air using lungs. Some frogs are still able to live and breathe underwater throughout their adult life. Frogs then reproduce by laying eggs in the water.

LADY BEETLE AND BUTTERFLY LIFE CYCLES

Lady Beetles, commonly called ladybugs and butterflies start their lives as eggs, which then hatch into a larva, which is most similar to a worm. In butterflies, this is called a caterpillar. The larva usually spends its life eating to build up energy for the change to its next stage. The larva eventually turns into a pupa or a chrysalis, which is a far less active stage. In this change, the larva spins a web around itself, becoming a cocoon. In this stage, the body changes form and eventually, an adult butterfly or ladybug emerges. The adult forms of both of these creatures have wings and are then able to fly and eventually produce new eggs.

CRICKET LIFE CYCLE

Crickets undergo a similar but far less dramatic lifecycle change than metamorphosing insects. They start as eggs, which hatch into **nymph** crickets, which are essentially the same as the adult form of the insect, only smaller and not capable of reproducing yet. As the nymph grows, it eventually comes into adulthood and can then mate and lay eggs.

PLATE TECTONICS

Earthquakes result from the movement of a dozen or so major lithospheric (crustal) plates that float upon Earth's mantle (asthenosphere). These **plates** move about each other in response to complex convection cells set in motion by Earth's interior heat. Two plates move apart from each other at divergent boundaries, or spreading centers, and come together at convergent boundaries. When thin, denser, iron- and magnesium- rich oceanic crust collides with thicker, lighter, silica-rich continental crust, the former is subducted beneath the latter. The subducted material carries scraped-off continental crust and seawater down with it. As this material melts, it rises as a mixture of magma and steam to produce explosive volcanic mountain ranges such as those surrounding the Pacific Ocean Basin. When two continental plates collide at convergent boundaries, the crust buckles and thrusts up massive mountain ranges such as the Alps and Himalayas.

RECORD OF THE EARTH'S HISTORY

ROCKS

One important way in which rocks provide a record of **earth's history** is through the study of **fossils**, which allows scientists to make inferences about the evolution of life on earth. However, the presentation of fossils is certainly not the only record of earth's history contained in rocks. For instance, the **chemical composition** of rock strata may give indications about the atmospheric and/or hydrospheric compositions at certain points in earth's history. Paleomagnetism constitutes another aspect of earth's historical record contained in rocks. Through the study of magnetic orientations of rocks formed at certain times in history, scientists learn more about the form and function of earth's magnetic field then and now.

SEDIMENTS

The study of the **sediments** which make up sedimentary rocks can reveal much about the environment in which they are formed. For example, a study of the **different types** of sediments in a bed, and the **ratios** in which they occur, can indicate the types of rocks exposed at the origination site and the relative abundances of each. Examination of the sorting of a sediment can reveal information about how far the particles traveled from their provenance, as well as the medium which carried the particles. For example, sediments transported by wind tend to be well-sorted, while water moves large particles which are often worn into spheres. The type of weathering experienced by particles in a sedimentary bed can reveal the climate from which they came— mechanical weathering tends to occur in cold and arid climates, while chemical weathering is more common in hot and humid climates. Interpreting the information supplied by sediment can, in turn, reveal information about past conditions on earth.

SOIL

The study of **soil development** can give indications of the **age of certain sedimentary deposits**. For example, the study of soil led to the idea that multiple glaciations have occurred on the North American continent. Examination of the development level of certain areas of soil can also inform earth scientists about natural catastrophic events which have occurred in the past. Study of soil deposits also aided in the determination of how often "ice ages" can be expected to occur. Also, the presence of certain types of soil buried deep beneath the surface can provide indications of past climates.

PREHISTORIC OCEANS

The elements present in the earliest oceans were quite different from those present in the Earth's hydrosphere today. This is largely due to the chemical composition of the atmosphere at that time. The oceans were formed when cooling caused atmospheric clouds to condense and produce rain.

Volcanic gasses contributed elements such as sulfur and carbon dioxide to the air. Therefore, scientists suspect that the earliest oceans contained high levels of acids (for example, sulfuric acid, hydrochloric acid, and hydrofluoric acid), and low levels of the salts that inhabit the oceans today. The temperature in this early ocean was probably close to 100 degrees Celsius. As **carbon dioxide** began to dissolve in the water, it combined with carbonate ions to form limestone which was deposited on the ocean floor. Consequently, more carbon dioxide was trapped in these rocks. Eventually, **calcium carbonate** began to reduce the acidity of these early oceans. **Weathering** brought different minerals into the ocean, which began to increase its saltiness toward its current levels.

RADIOMETRIC DATING

Radiometric dating is one of the only methods currently available to determine the absolute age of an object such as a fossil or rock body. This process is possible when such an object contains isotopes, the products of radioactive decay. In radioactive decay, the atoms of certain unstable isotopes are transformed through the emissions of either electrons or alpha particles. This process occurs exponentially until it produces a stable final product. The rate of radioactive decay is measured in half-lives: after one half-life has passed, one-half of the atoms of the original element will have decayed. When scientists examine an object which contains isotopes with known half-life periods, they can determine the amount of the isotope that was present at the time of the object's origin. That figure can then be compared with the present level to determine the age of the object.

GAIA HYPOTHESIS

Named for the Greek goddess who organized a living earth from chaos, the **Gaia hypothesis** states that the planet is a **living system**. While this idea is not scientific in the literal sense, it provides a metaphor which is useful in achieving an understanding of the interconnectedness of all of earth's systems. For example, increased levels of carbon dioxide in the atmosphere breed higher levels of plant growth, and these plants help to regulate the amount of carbon dioxide present in the atmosphere. Feedback mechanisms such as this were known before the formulation of the Gaia hypothesis. However, adherence to this idea requires one to study the planet as a whole, rather than focusing on only one of its many aspects in isolation. The fact that earth's atmosphere is quite different from those of the other planets led to the formulation of this idea.

PALEONTOLOGY

Paleontology is the study of ancient plant and animal life. The bulk of information on this subject is provided by the fossil record, which consists of fossilized plants, animals, tracks, and chemical residues preserved in rock strata. There are three general subdivisions within the field of paleontology. The first, **paleozoology**, is the study of ancient animal life, including vertebrate and invertebrate specializations, as well as paleoanthropology, the study of fossil hominids. The second is **paleobotany**, the study of ancient plant life. The third, **micropaleontology**, is the study of microfossils. This field of scientific inquiry is useful in identifying the evolutionary processes that gave rise to present-day life forms. Paleontology also contributes to an understanding of the ways that environmental and geological factors affected evolution.

THEORY OF EVOLUTION

Evolution is the theoretical process whereby organisms pass certain acquired traits to successive generations, affecting the attributes of later organisms and even leading to the creation of new species. Charles Darwin is the name often associated with the formulation of natural selection, a vital component of evolution as it is known today. **Natural selection** states that members of a species are not identical—due to their respective genetic make-ups, each individual will possess traits which make it stronger or weaker and more or less able to adapt. The other tenet of natural selection is that members of a species will always have to compete for scarce resources to survive. Therefore, organisms with traits which will help them survive are more likely to do so and produce offspring, passing along the "desirable" traits. Darwin suggested that this process, by creating groups of a species with increasingly different characteristics, would eventually lead to the formation of **a new species**.

FOSSILS

Fossils are the preserved remains or traces of animals, plants, and other organisms from the remote past. These remains may consist of mineralized parts, of impressions left in sediment, or even of entire carcasses. All known fossils make up the fossil record. Scientists use this record to learn about life on ancient Earth and the evolutionary processes which led to life on Earth as it is today. To glean any valuable information from a fossil, scientists must make an attempt to understand the preservation history of a specimen; they must examine the process by which the specimen became a fossil and the natural forces to which it was subjected after fossilization. While certain elements of an organism such as teeth and bone are fairly durable, soft tissues like eyes and skin decay quickly after death. Therefore, to be preserved, an organism must be buried in sediment soon after its death. Since the majority of sediments are deposited on the sea floor, most fossils are preserved marine animals.

TYPES OF FOSSILS

On rare occasions, full carcasses of animals are frozen in permafrost terrain, such as the wooly mammoths discovered in Siberia. This type of fossil provides scientists with a wealth of information about an organism because details such as the organism's soft tissue, blood cells, and hints of digested food remain intact. Similarly, small insects may become trapped in tree resin which later hardens into amber, preserving the entire insect. Small bodies may also be preserved when sedimentary concretions form around them. Durable parts of organisms, such as bones, teeth, and shells, may be fossilized when they are buried by sediment soon after the death of the organism. These fragments experience diagenesis with the sediment around them and are preserved. **Permineralization** is the process whereby minerals (such as calcium phosphate or silica) intrude the pore space of an organism's skeleton. Mould fossils or typolites are created when the dissolution of carcasses leave an impression in rock. Trace fossils are impressions left in rock by the movement of an organism, such as footprints or subsurface dwellings.

Practice Test #1

Practice Questions

1. In a science experiment, a student is asked to identify the freezing and melting points of water. Which piece of laboratory equipment should be used?

    a. Balance
    b. Thermometer
    c. Ruler
    d. Graduated cylinder

2. In the diagram shown below, four wheels are in contact such that each wheel turns the opposite direction from the wheels it is touching. Wheel A is being turned clockwise by a force as shown. Which statement about wheel D is correct?

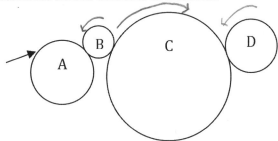

    a. Wheel D does not turn at all because there are too many wheels between it and wheel A
    b. Wheel D does not turn at all because it is not touching wheel C
    c. Wheel D turns counterclockwise
    d. Wheel D turns clockwise

3. The United States is divided into four time zones. The east coast is three hours ahead of the west coast. This means that when it is 6:00pm in New York, on the east coast, it is 3:00pm in California on the west coast. Based on the information given, which direction does Earth rotate on its axis?

    a. Clockwise as viewed from above the north pole
    b. Counterclockwise as viewed from above the north pole
    c. Toward the Sun
    d. The direction varies depending on the season

4. A boy is outside in the winter and notices that he begins shivering when he gets cold. A girl is outside during the summer and begins sweating when she gets hot. Why do the children's bodies react this way?

    a. The children's bodies are attempting to regulate their temperature
    b. The children's bodies are trying to fight off disease
    c. The children's bodies are reacting to the amount of sunlight or shade
    d. The children are having an allergic reaction to something in the air

5. How does the tilt of Earth's axis cause seasons?

    a.   A hemisphere experiences winter when that half of Earth is tilted away from the Sun. It experiences summer when that half of Earth is tilted towards the Sun

    b.   A hemisphere experiences spring when that half of Earth is tilted away from the Sun. It experiences autumn when that half of Earth is tilted towards the Sun

    c.   A hemisphere experiences summer when that half of Earth is tilted away from the Sun. It experiences winter when that half of Earth is tilted towards the Sun

    d.   A hemisphere experiences autumn when that half of Earth is tilted away from the Sun. It experiences spring when that half of Earth is tilted towards the Sun

Power Fruit	
All natural fruit juice that gives you energy all day long	
35 mg of Caffeine	9% DV
100 mg of Vitamin C	110% DV

6. The advertisement above shows the nutrition information for the new juice, "Power Fruit". Which conclusion can be made about Power Fruit?

    a.   Power Fruit contains the daily value of caffeine

    b.   Power Fruit provides all the vitamin C you need each day

    c.   Power Fruit has 100% daily value of vitamin A

    d.   Power Fruit does not contain iron

7. Which of the following sources of fresh water is unavailable for human use?

    a.   Rivers

    b.   Estuaries

    c.   Aquifers

    d.   Glaciers

8. How are igneous rocks formed?

    a.   Years of sediment are laid down on top of each other and forced together

    b.   Acid rain caused by pollution creates holes in metamorphic rocks

    c.   Dust and pebbles are pressed together underground from Earth's heat and pressure

    d.   Magma from a volcanic eruption cools and hardens

9. Jim and John are working on their science fair project when they accidently break a beaker. What should the boys do?

    a.   Tell their teacher immediately

    b.   Clean up the broken glass themselves

    c.   Move away from the broken glass and continue working

    d.   Hide the broken glass so they don't get in trouble

10. Why do balloons filled with helium float while balloons filled with air do not float?

   a. Balloons filled with air are larger than balloons filled with helium, which makes them heavier preventing them from floating
   b. Helium is less dense than air, which allows balloons filled with helium to float
   c. Helium balloons travel on higher air currents and balloons filled with air travel on lower air currents
   d. Air causes balloons to generate static electricity so the balloon will be attracted to the ground

11. Which of the following is the most likely food source for a carnivore?

   a. A plant
   b. The Sun
   c. An animal
   d. A dead tree

12. Why are plants considered producers?

   a. They make their own food
   b. They soak up water from the ground
   c. Their leaves can be large or small
   d. They produce pollen, which is a food source for many insects and birds

13. How should students determine the volume of fluid in a graduated cylinder?

   a. Read the volume at the bottom of the meniscus
   b. Read the volume at the highest point the fluid reaches
   c. Read the volume at the center, between the meniscus and the highest point of the fluid
   d. Read the volume at the highest point then round to the nearest tens

14. A student is conducting an experiment using a ball that is attached to the end of a string on a pendulum. The student pulls the ball back so that it is at an angle to its resting position. As the student releases the ball, it swings forward and backward. The student measures the time it takes the ball to make one complete period. A period is defined as the time it takes the ball to swing forward and back again to its starting position. This is repeated using different string lengths.

   The student formed the following hypothesis: *Lengthening the string of the pendulum increases the time it takes the ball to make one complete period.*

What correction would you have the student make to the hypothesis?

   a. Turn it into an "if/then" statement
   b. Add the word "will" in the middle after the word "pendulum"
   c. Switch the order of the sentence so that the phrase about the period comes first, and the phrase about the string's length is last
   d. No corrections are needed

15. When should instructions for a laboratory experiment be read?

   a. Instructions only need to be read if the teacher does not explain the steps of the lab well
   b. The instructions should be read if the students get confused or are not sure of the steps in the lab
   c. Instructions should be read thoroughly before beginning the lab
   d. The instructions do not need to be read, they are only a suggestion for how to complete the lab

16. A ball is thrown and the distance it traveled is measured. Which data set corresponds to the graph below?

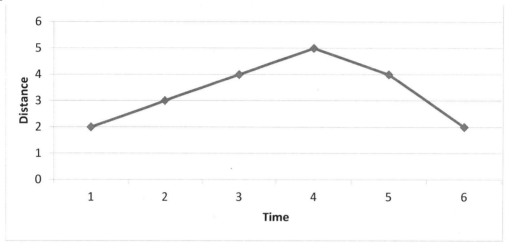

a.

Time	Distance
1	2
2	4
3	6
4	8
5	9

c.

Time	Distance
2	0
4	1
6	3
8	5
9	7

b.

Time	Distance
1	2
3	4
5	6
7	8
9	9

d.

Time	Distance
1	2
2	3
3	4
4	5
5	4
6	2

17. The data below was collected by repeating the same experiment four different times. What conclusion can be drawn based on the data shown?

Bicycle Obstacle Race

Student	Trial 1	Trial 2	Trial 3	Trial 4
Kayla	57.6 s	37.6 s	37.3 s	36.2 s
Carson	64.0 s	32.6 s	31.2 s	28.4 s
Jeremy	59.2 s	31.0 s	28.8 s	27.9 s
Rachel	61.3 s	42.6 s	39.5 s	39.0 s

a.   The data was accurate in all four trials
b.   The data in trials 2 through 4 is probably inaccurate
c.   An error occurred in trial 1 that gave inaccurate data
d.   The times in trial 4 are fastest because the students were tired

18. The first microscope was developed by Hans and Zacharias Janssen and allowed scientists to

    a. See organisms too small to be seen with the naked eye
    b. Count the number of organisms in the universe
    c. Determine the causes of all human illness
    d. Study why some females are taller than others

19. Electrical cords, such as the cords of a television or the cord on a toaster, are covered with rubber or plastic. What would you expect to happen if a portion of the rubber covering were missing when you tried to plug the cord in?

    a. The appliance would not work after it was plugged in
    b. The person plugging the appliance in would feel an electric shock
    c. The appliance being plugged in would work, but all other appliances in the home would stop working
    d. The cover does not matter, all appliances would work normally

20. Which of the statements below explains why a boy can run fast on the beach, but is much slower in water?

    a. The boy is afraid of sharks and slows down when he enters the water
    b. The boy cannot swim and stops running to avoid drowning
    c. Water is thicker than air, which creates more resistance and slows the boy down
    d. The force of the waves causes the boy to float, which prevents him from running

21. Place your answer on the provided griddable answer sheet.

In order to produce a constant supply of energy, solar panels require constant exposure to what?

22. Which statement accurately describes a state of matter?

    a. Solids take the shape of their container
    b. Gases maintain a fixed shape
    c. Liquids will expand to fill the volume of a container
    d. Gases expand to fill an entire space

23. Based on the weather forecast, what can a farmer expect to happen to his bird bath overnight?

10pm	11pm	12am	1am	2am	3am	4am	5am
34°C	25°C	11°C	2°C	-4 °C	-12 °C	-18°C	-18°C

    a. Freeze
    b. Evaporate
    c. Melt
    d. Sublime

24. The boiling point of water is 100°C. Adding salt raises the boiling point. What is the result of adding salt to water when cooking pasta?

    a. The pasta cooks more slowly
    b. The pasta will not stick together
    c. The water will boil more quickly
    d. The pasta will cook in hotter water

25. A man accidentally drops his wallet in a swimming pool. He can see his wallet at the bottom of the pool. He jumps in to retrieve it, but the wallet is not where it appeared to be. What is the reason for the optical illusion?

    a. The reflection of sunlight off of the water disrupted his view
    b. Light is refracted as it enters the water changing the wallet's apparent location
    c. The current at the bottom of the pool caused the wallet to move
    d. The heat from the Sun has impaired the man's vision

26. Two students spent several hours testing how well different running shoes supported athletes' feet. All of the following allow the students to effectively communicate the results of their experiment except

    a. Create an advertisement that tells only the positive results of the shoes
    b. Design a side by side comparison with graphs and conclusions that reveals all of the results of the experiment
    c. Develop an oral report that presents their results
    d. Write a paper that summarizes their experiment and results

27. The observations outlined below were made about a pot of water over a campfire. What is the most likely explanation for these observations?

The pot was half full of water
The pot hung over the campfire for 15 minutes
The water began boiling after 7 minutes
A white vapor was observed over the pot
After 15 minutes, the pot was one quarter of the way full

    a. Some of the water disappeared
    b. The water changes from a gas to a liquid
    c. Some of the water changed from a liquid to a gas, which was the vapor observed
    d. The pot was never half full, someone measured incorrectly

28. A ball is resting on the front end of a boat. The boat is moving straight forwards toward a dock. When the front of the boat hits the dock, how will the ball's motion change?

    a. The ball will remain at rest
    b. The ball will move backwards
    c. The ball will move forwards
    d. The ball will move sideways

29. Which statement describes how fossil fuels are made?

    a. Oil from Earth's core slowly rises to the Earth's surface and forms ponds
    b. Lava within some volcanoes becomes so hot that is transforms into fossil fuels
    c. Dead and decomposing organisms, exposed to extreme heat and pressure, transform into fossil fuels
    d. When mountains form on top of coal, the pressure liquefies the coal creating fossil fuels

30. The Sahara desert receives about 3.6 inches of precipitation per year. Antarctica is also a desert receiving between 3 to 8 inches of precipitation per year. What makes an area a desert?

   a. The temperature
   b. The amount of animal life
   c. The number of people living in the region
   d. The yearly precipitation

31. What question are the students most likely testing with the experiment outlined below?

Seed type: Pansy	Seed type: Pansy	Seed type: Pansy
Water: ½ gallon daily	Water: ½ gallon daily	Water: ½ gallon daily
Soil: Bob's soil	Soil: Texas dirt	Soil: Grow Up Dirt
Daylight: 3 hours per day	Daylight: 3 hours per day	Daylight: 3 hours per day
Flower color: Blue	Flower color: Purple	Flower color: red

   a. Does the amount of water affect how tall a flower will grow?
   b. Does the type of soil affect the color of a flower?
   c. What color of flower do bees prefer?
   d. Is three hours of daylight enough for flowers to grow?

32. A prairie ecosystem is described below. Which organisms from the ecosystem are carnivores?

Grass is eaten by grasshoppers, rabbits, and crickets
Corn is eaten by squirrels and beetles
Grasshoppers, beetles, and crickets are all eaten by birds
Squirrels, birds, and rabbits are all eaten by both foxes and coyotes

   a. Corn and grass
   b. Grasshoppers and crickets
   c. Beetles and birds
   d. Foxes and coyotes

33. In a food chain, where does energy go after the secondary consumer dies?

   a. Back to the Sun
   b. To the producers
   c. Into air, becomes wind
   d. To decomposers

34. Every year thousands of square miles of trees are cut down to make paper products. Which of the following is not a result of cutting down trees?

   a. Animals experience a loss of habitat
   b. There is a decrease in the amount of oxygen available
   c. There is a decrease in the amount of food available to herbivores and omnivores
   d. There is a decrease in the amount of CO_2 in the atmosphere

35. According to the data below, what can be determined about Saturn?

Planet	Length of Year	Length of Day
Venus	224.7 days	116.75 days
Earth	365 days	24 hours
Saturn	10,759 days	10 hours 32 minutes
Neptune	164.79 years	16.11 hours

a. Saturn takes the least amount of time to rotate on its axis.
b. Saturn is the furthest planet from the Sun.
c. The further a planet is from the Sun, the shorter its day will be.
d. The larger a planet is, the longer its day will be.

36. A dog is an omnivore. What would you expect a dog's diet to consist of?

a. Meat
b. Vegetables
c. Both meat and vegetables
d. Neither meat nor vegetables

37. The following represents a simple food chain. What trophic level contains the greatest amount of energy?

$$tree \rightarrow caterpillar \rightarrow frog \rightarrow snake \rightarrow hawk \rightarrow worm$$

a. tree
b. caterpillar
c. hawk
d. worm

38. How are organisms, such as snakes, cacti, and coyotes, able to survive in harsh desert conditions?

a. Over thousands of years these organisms have developed adaptations to survive in arid climates
b. These organisms migrate out of the desert during the summer months, only living in the desert for a portion of the year
c. Snakes, cacti, and coyotes work together to find sources of food and water
d. Snakes, cacti, and coyotes are all aquatic species that live in ponds and rivers during the hot day

39. A student is building a model of the Solar System using produce from the local supermarket. What order should she put the objects in to correctly represent the Solar System?

Object in Solar System	Model	Object in Solar System	Model
Mars	Raspberry	Uranus	tomato
Saturn	Grapefruit	Mercury	raisin
The Sun	Watermelon	Venus	grape
Jupiter	Lettuce	Asteroid Belt	sunflower seeds
Earth	Cherry	Neptune	orange

a. Watermelon-raisin-grape-cherry-raspberry-tomato-orange-lettuce-grapefruit-seeds
b. Watermelon-raisin-grape-cherry-raspberry-seeds-lettuce-grapefruit-tomato-orange
c. Watermelon-lettuce-grapefruit-tomato-orange-cherry-grape-raspberry-raisin-seeds
d. Watermelon-grape-raisin-cherry-seeds-raspberry-lettuce-grapefruti-orange-tomato

40. Why is it important to form a hypothesis before performing an experiment?

    a. The experimenter will not have enough time to create a hypothesis after beginning the experiment

    b. Developing a hypothesis ensures that the lab will be safe

    c. The experiment will take too much time to complete if there is no hypothesis

    d. The hypothesis tells what the experiment is going to be testing

41. A student is working on a science project and is going through each step of the scientific method. After the student conducts his or her first experiment and records the results of the experimental test, what should the student do next?

    a. Communicate the results

    b. Draw a conclusion

    c. Repeat the experiment

    d. Create a hypothesis

42. Which of the following is considered a non-renewable resource?

    a. Glass

    b. Wood

    c. Cattle

    d. Soil

43. How is force being applied to the box below?

    a. The box is being pulled forward

    b. The box is being pushed forward

    c. Gravity is forcing the box to move forward

    d. Friction is forcing the box to stop

44. What is the benefit of a kangaroo's large ears?

    a. They improve the kangaroo's vision

    b. Large ears help kangaroos taste their food

    c. Large ears allow kangaroos to outrun predators

    d. Large ears help kangaroos hear predators coming

Answers and Explanations

1. B: Thermometers are used to measure temperature. Graduated cylinders are used to measure volume while a ruler is used to measure distance. Balances are used to measure mass.

2. C: Wheel A is turning clockwise, which causes wheel B to turn counterclockwise. Wheel B then causes wheel C to turn clockwise. Wheel C in turn, turns wheel D in the counterclockwise direction. The question states that the wheels are in contact, and the number of intermediate wheels does not prevent the turning motion from being transferred all the way down the line.

3. B: The east coast, states such as Maine, New York, and New Hampshire are three hours ahead of states on the west coast such as California, Washington, and Oregon. Earth rotates west to east, and that is counterclockwise when viewed from above the North Pole.

4. A: The human body works best within a certain temperature range, around 98.6°F. When the body gets too cold or too hot it cannot function properly. The boy who is outside in the winter is cold. His body temperature is dropping below 98.6°F. His muscles start to contract causing him to shiver in order to generate heat. The girl is outside in the summer, and begins sweating to reduce her body temperature from rising too far above 98.6°F. In both cases, the children's bodies are trying to keep the temperature close to 98.6°F.

5. A: Heat on Earth is generated by the Sun. The more direct sunlight an area on Earth receives from the Sun, the warmer it will be. When the Northern hemisphere is tilted away from the Sun, all of the countries in the Northern hemisphere experience winter. At that same time, the Southern hemisphere experiences summer. The same is true when the Southern hemisphere experiences winter; the Northern hemisphere experiences summer.

6. B: The advertisement states that Power Fruit contains 100% of the daily value of vitamin C, which means that it meets the amount of vitamin C a person needs each day. The ad also states that Power Fruit contains 35 mg of caffeine, but there is no indication of what the daily value of caffeine is. There is no mention of vitamin A or iron anywhere in the advertisement.

7. D: Glaciers and ice caps are fresh water unavailable for human use as they are frozen. The hydrologic cycle refers to all the water on planet Earth. Some water is in forms that humans do not tend to use, such as oceans (too salty and expensive to desalinate) and glaciers. Water suitable for drinking can be found as surface water and in ground water, which is obtained through wells. Answers A, Rivers, B, Estuaries, and C, Aquifers, are all examples of surface water that are available to humans.

8. D: Igneous rocks are formed when magma in Earth erupts through cracks in the crust where it cools creating a hard structure with many air pockets or holes.

9. A: Anytime there is an accident in the lab, the first step is always to tell the teacher. Even if a student or students were doing something that they should not have been doing, such as horse playing in the lab, the teacher's first priority is still to make sure the students are safe. Telling the teacher will allow him or her to respond appropriately to the situation and make sure that all of the students remain safe.

10. B: The air we breathe is composed of many types of molecules, and is quite heavy compared to helium. The reason helium balloons float is because helium is less dense than the surrounding air. Objects that are less dense will float in objects that are more dense, as a helium balloon does when surrounded by air.

11. C: The prefix *carni-* means flesh, so carnivores are flesh eaters. Their diet consists of meats. The only answer choice that is a meat is an animal.

12. A: Plants are considered producers because they are able to absorb light energy from the Sun and convert it into food through the process of photosynthesis. In other words, plants are producers because they produce their own food from sunlight.

13. A: The volume of a graduated cylinder should be read at the bottom of the meniscus.

14. A: Turn it into an "if/then" statement. A formalized hypothesis written in the form of an if/then statement can then be tested. A statement may make a prediction or imply a cause/effect relationship, but that does not necessarily make it a good hypothesis. In this example, having the student rewrite the statement in the form of an if/then statement could read: If the length of the string of the pendulum is varied, then the time it takes the ball to make one complete period changes. This hypothesis is testable, doesn't simply make a prediction, nor does it give a conclusion. The validity of the hypothesis can then be supported or disproved by experimentation and observation.

15. C: Laboratory instructions not only contain steps to the procedure, but also often contain important safety information. The instructions should always be read before beginning the lab. Any questions should be addressed by the instructor before starting an experiment.

16. D: The graph represents a set of data. The line graph increases in distance from 1 second to 4 seconds and then begins decreasing. The only data set that shows distance increasing and then decreasing is set D.

17. C: The data is relatively consistent with the exception of trial 1. When an experiment is repeated using the same process multiple times, the data from each trial should be very similar or the same. The results of trial 1 indicate that an error may have occurred in the procedure yielding inaccurate results.

18. A: The microscope was discovered when a series of lenses were placed in a specific order magnifying objects that were too small to see otherwise. The development of the microscope also led to discoveries such as the cell, bacteria, and fungi.

19. B: The purpose of the rubber coating on the outside of electrical cords is to contain the electric current in the metal wire. When part of the rubber coating is missing, the electric current can leave the wire and cause an electric shock to the person plugging in the wire.

20. C: Water is denser than air and creates more resistance on the boy running. Air is thin and this allows the boy to run fast on the beach.

21. Sun: The word *solar* refers to the sun. Solar panels are large panels that absorb energy from the sun and convert it into other types of energy, such as electrical energy, that can be used to power anything from a car to a toaster. If there is no sun, such as at night, the panels do not take in any solar energy to convert to electricity. The amount of energy each solar panel can produce depends on the amount of sunlight it is exposed to.

22. D: The molecules that make up gases are far apart and move about very quickly. Because they have a weak attraction to each other, they expand to take up as much space as possible.

23. A: The weather forecast shows that a cold front will be arriving in the area causing the temperature to drop from 34°C to -18°C. The freezing point of water is 0°C, which means that the water in the birdbath will freeze overnight after the cold front arrives.

24. D: Adding salt to water causes the boiling point of water to rise. The water has to reach a temperature beyond 100°C in order to boil, so the water will be hotter when the pasta cooks. It is a common misconception that because the salt water is boiling at a higher temperature, the pasta will cook faster. The increase in temperature is too slight to make a significant difference in cooking time.

25. B: Light travels faster in air than it can in water. Water molecules are closer together than air particles are, which causes the light to slow down and bend as it enters the water. The bending of light is called refraction and creates the illusion of the wallet being next to where it actually is.

26. A: The purpose of a scientific experiment is to collect as much reliable data as possible about a specific hypothesis. Scientists can use the results from other experiments to help them determine what hypothesis to test next. Creating an advertisement that tells only the positive aspects of the running shoes would omit any negative aspects of the shoes that may be relevant. The results would not be reliable because they would be incomplete.

27. C: Water boils at 100°C. As the pot of water heats up over the campfire, it begins to boil causing the liquid water to turn into water vapor, a gas. The vapor the campers observed over the boiling pot of water was water vapor. As the water continues to boil, more of the liquid turns into gas resulting in a decrease in the volume of water in the pot.

28. C: The ball will move forwards. The ball is moving forward with the boat. When the front of the boat hits the dock, the ball's motion does not change. It continues to move forward because the force acting to stop the boat is not acting upon the ball. The forward motion of the boat is halted by the dock. The forward motion of the ball is not stopped. Since the ball is round there is little friction to provide an equal and opposite reaction to the forward motion.

29. C: Organisms that lived millions of years ago have been covered up by many layers of earth. The temperature and pressure increases transforming the dead organisms into fossil fuels that can be obtained and used for energy.

30. D: A desert is classified by the average amount of precipitation the region receives on a yearly basis. The temperature is irrelevant, as there are both hot and cold deserts. Due to the dry conditions, only organisms designed to withstand the arid conditions can survive in these areas.

31. B: In order to determine the question being tested, you must look at the data given. Answer choice A asks about how tall a flower will grow, but the height of the flowers is not given, so this cannot be what was tested. Answer choice C asks about bees, which are also not referenced anywhere in the experiment. Answer choice D asks about the amount of daylight required for the flowers to grow. All three flowers were given the same amount of daylight- three hours, so this cannot be what is tested. The only change between each of the tests is the type of dirt used, which affected the flower color.

32. D: Carnivores eat meat only. In the ecosystem described, both coyotes and foxes are carnivores eating squirrels, birds, and rabbits.

33. D: After a secondary consumer dies, such as a wolf, its body is partially consumed by decomposers, such as bacteria and fungi. Bacteria and fungi live in soil and digest body tissues of dead organisms converting them into basic nutrients that plants need to grow. Therefore, after secondary consumers die, their energy is consumed by decomposers, who make nutrients available in the soil for producers to use. *Do not confuse nutrients in the soil with energy that producers get from the Sun to make their own food.*

34. D: Trees absorb and use carbon dioxide to produce their own food. Humans breathe in oxygen and breathe out carbon dioxide. To a human, too much carbon dioxide is toxic and can cause serious problems. Plants use carbon dioxide and release oxygen as waste. This allows what is toxic to humans, carbon dioxide, to be used and transformed into breathable oxygen. A decrease in the number of trees decreases the amount of plants taking in carbon dioxide, causing the carbon dioxide levels in the atmosphere to rise.

35. A: When a planet rotates on its axis it creates day and night. The side of the planet that faces away from the Sun is in night. When that side rotates around to face the Sun, it is in day. The data indicates that Saturn takes the least amount of time to rotate on its axis, which indicates that is has the shortest day at only 10 hours and 32 minutes.

36. C: The prefix *omni-*means all, so an omnivore eats all types of food. Omnivores, such as dogs and many humans, eat a variety of plants and meats to achieve a balanced diet.

37. A: In the food chain of tree → caterpillar → frog → snake → hawk → worm, the tree is at the trophic level with the greatest amount of energy. Trophic level refers to the position of an organism in a food chain. Energy is lost according to the laws of thermodynamics as one moves up the food chain because it is converted to heat when consumers consume. Primary producers, such as autotrophs, are organisms who are at the base and capture solar energy. Primary consumers are herbivores that feed on the producers. Secondary consumers consume primary consumers and so on. Decomposers get their energy from the consumption of dead plants and animals.

38. A: Many organisms, especially organisms that live in harsh conditions such as deserts or frozen icy areas, have developed specific adaptations that allow them to survive. For example, cacti are able to expand to store large amounts of water, coyotes absorb some water from their food, and snakes can escape the heat by hiding within rocks.

39. B: This question is really asking you to determine the correct order of the major bodies in the Solar System. The correct order is: Sun (watermelon), Mercury (raisin), Venus (grape), Earth (cherry), Mars (raspberry), asteroid belt (seeds), Jupiter (lettuce), Saturn (grapefruit), Uranus (tomato), Neptune (orange).

40. D: A hypothesis predicts what the experimenter thinks is going to happen and why. It is based on prior knowledge and research. An experiment is designed to test the hypothesis. Without a hypothesis, an experiment cannot be designed or performed.

41. C: Repeating the experiment validates data. Each separate experiment is called a repetition. Results of experiments or tests should be able to be replicated. Similar data gathered from many experiments can also be used to quantify the validity of the hypothesis. Repeating the experiments allows the student to observe variation in the results. Variation in data can be caused by a variety of errors or may be disproving the hypothesis. Answer D, Create a hypothesis, comes before experiments. Answers A, Communicate the results, and B, Draw a conclusion, occur after testing.

42. A: Glass is considered a non-renewable resource. Glass is manufactured and can be recycled, but is considered a non-renewable resource. Answer B, Wood, is considered a renewable resource because with proper management, an equilibrium can be reached between harvesting trees and planting new ones. Cattle, Answer C, are managed in herds and a balance can be achieved between those consumed and those born. Answer D, Soil, is the result of long-term erosion and includes organic matter and minerals needed by plants. Soil found naturally in the environment is renewed. Crops can be rotated to help maintain a healthy soil composition for farming.

43. A: The picture shows an arrow in front of the box pulling the box forward. If the box were being pushed, the arrow would be behind the box pushing it forward. Gravity pulls downward, not forward.

44. D: Kangaroos live in a dry, wide-open environment where there is little coverage from predators. It is important for kangaroos to be able to hear predators coming from a far distance so they can escape. Their large ears help them to hear subtle sounds of potential predators from far away.

Practice Test #2

Practice Questions

1. A prairie ecosystem is described below. Farmers treat fields surrounding the prairie with pesticides that kill part of the beetle population. What effect would the pesticides have on the rest of the ecosystem?

Grass is eaten by grasshoppers, rabbits, and crickets
Corn is eaten by squirrels and beetles
Grasshoppers, beetles, and crickets are all eaten by birds
Squirrels, birds, and rabbits are all eaten by both foxes and coyotes

a. There would be a decrease in the cricket population.
b. There would be an increase in the population of birds.
c. The population of rabbits would decrease.
d. The population of foxes would increase.

2. Which organisms from the ecosystem described above are herbivores?

a. Corn and grass
b. Grasshoppers and crickets
c. Beetles and birds
d. Foxes and coyotes

3. Which statement correctly describes the relationship between plants and animals?

a. Animals breathe in oxygen and plants release oxygen.
b. Animals breathe in carbon dioxide while plants release carbon dioxide.
c. Animals breathe in carbon dioxide while plants breathe out carbon dioxide.
d. Animals get oxygen from plants by eating the plants.

77

4. Which picture best represents Earth's position on its axis?

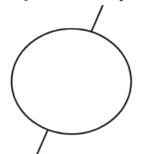

a.

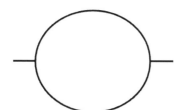

b.

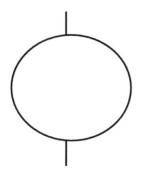

c.

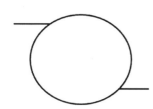

d.

5. What should be included in a hypothesis?

a. A hypothesis should tell what you think is going to happen and why.
b. A hypothesis should state what the results of similar experiments were.
c. A hypothesis should summarize the results of an experiment.
d. A hypothesis should compare the control to the variable.

6. What causes high and low tide?

a. The Earth's rotation
b. The Moon's gravity
c. The wind currents
d. The change in water temperature

7. Earth rotates on its axis every 24 hours and revolves around the Sun every 365 earth days. Mars revolves around the Sun every 687 earth days. What does a period 687 earth days represent in terms of Mars time?

   a. One Martian day
   b. One Martian year
   c. One Martian season
   d. One Martian month

8. What does a food chain show?

   a. The flow of energy between organisms
   b. Very type of species living in a habitat
   c. The population of each species in a habitat
   d. The number of offspring a species will produce in a year

9. Lions live in savannah and grassland regions where there are tall dry grasses. Lions must sneak up and stalk their prey. What is the most likely reason for a lion's sand colored coat?

   a. It allows lions to hide within the grass
   b. The light color of their coat reflects heat from the Sun
   c. A lion's coloring helps it attract mates
   d. It allows them to run faster than their prey

10. In which of the following scenarios is Mario not applying work to a book?

   a. Mario moves a book from the floor to the top shelf of a bookcase
   b. Mario lets go of a book that he is holding so that it falls to the floor
   c. Mario pushes a box of books across the room
   d. Mario balances a book on his head and walks across the room

11. Wind farms are one source of alternative energy, energy that can be used in place of fossil fuels. The amount of energy a wind farm produces is determined by

   a. Sunlight
   b. Season
   c. Wind
   d. Rainfall

12. A carnivore would eat all of the following except

   a. Rabbits
   b. Acorns
   c. Fish
   d. Deer

13. What instrument should be used to measure how fast a boy can run 100 meters?

   a. Beaker
   b. Meterstick
   c. Stopwatch
   d. Thermometer

14. Students have just completed a lab. What can they do to be sure that their results are reliable?

   a. Repeat the lab again
   b. Compare their data to data collected in similar experiments
   c. Measure all of their results twice with two different rulers
   d. Make sure that their results confirm that their hypothesis was correct

15. What would be the best material to make a cooking pot out of?

   a. Rubber
   b. Copper
   c. Plastic
   b. Cement

16. Flowers, trees, and shrubs are all examples of what?

   a. Carnivores
   b. Herbivores
   c. Producers
   d. Predators

17. Why can a person see their reflection in a mirror?

   a. Light is scattered when it hits a mirror producing a backward image
   b. Light is reflected off of the mirror back towards the person standing in front of it
   c. Light bends as it passes through the mirror creating an optical illusion
   d. Light is refracted, which produces a mirror image behind the glass

18. A tropical flower is planted in a local garden. The garden is watered 2 to 3 times per week during all seasons. After only a few months the tropical plant begins to droop and turn brown. How did environmental change most likely affect the tropical plant?

   a. Being watered 2 to 3 times per week was not enough to sustain a tropical plant
   b. The new environment was too hot and burned the plant
   c. Insects attacked the plant causing it to wilt
   d. The new soil lacked the nutrients necessary to maintain the plant's health

19. Place your answer on the provided griddable answer sheet.

How many planets are in Earth's solar system?

20. What type of satellite is Pluto?

   a. Planet
   b. Comet
   c. Dwarf planet Boo
   d. Asteroid

21. Algae are part of many food chains. How do algae produce energy?

   algae   fish   seal   shark

   a. They hunt fish for food
   b. Algae undergo photosynthesis
   c. They decompose dead or dying organisms
   d. They consume fossil fuel from beneath Earth's surface

22. Four windows are washed with different cleaners. The same paper towel is used on each. The squares below show each window before being cleaned. What is the variable in the experiment?

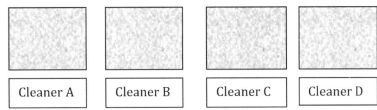

Cleaner A	Cleaner B	Cleaner C	Cleaner D

    a. The amount of sunlight coming through the windows
    b. The type of window cleaner used
    c. The amount of dirt on each window
    d. The type of paper towel used

23. Why is it more difficult to push a shopping cart full of groceries than an empty shopping cart?
    a. The full cart has less mass than the empty cart
    b. The full cart has a greater mass than the empty cart
    c. The full cart has less friction than the empty cart
    d. The empty cart is not pulled down by gravity

24. Use the information in the table to determine what would happen to the mass and weight of a human if he or she were on Neptune.

Mass	Mass is the amount of matter there is. Mass only changes when matter is added or removed.
Weight	Weight is how much gravity pulls downward on an object. The more gravity there is, the more an object weighs.
Gravity on Earth: 9.8 m/s^2	Gravity on Neptune: 11.15 m/s^2

    a. A person's mass and weight would increase on Neptune
    b. A person's mass and weight would decrease on Neptune
    c. A person's mass would increase, but weight would be unchanged
    d. A person's mass would be unchanged, but weight would increase

25. Look at the two images of a spring shown below. The first is a spring before it has been stretched by a force. The second is the same spring after it has been stretched by a force. Use your ruler to determine how far the force caused the spring to stretch?

Before Force

After force

    a. 0.2 cm
    b. 0.5 cm
    c. 1.0 cm
    d. 1.5 cm

26. How are the size of a dog and the pitch of its bark related?

Breed	Height from ground to back	Pitch of Bark
Chihuahua	20 cm	17 Hz
Cocker Spaniel	45 cm	14 Hz
Labrador	63 cm	12 Hz
Dalmatian	78 cm	11 Hz
Great Dane	114 cm	8 Hz

    a. The smaller breeds have a lower pitch bark than the larger breeds
    b. The size of the dog has no relationship to the pitch of the bark
    c. The larger breeds have a lower pitch bark than the smaller breeds
    d. The smallest breed and largest breed have the highest pitch barks

27. How are we able to see the Moon on a dark night?

    a. The Moon reflects light from the Sun, which illuminates the Moon
    b. The Moon generates energy that makes it glow
    c. The Moon reflects heat from the Sun that causes it to glow
    d. The Moon's surface is covered in active volcanoes that glow when they erupt

28. In the diagram shown below, four wheels are in contact such that each wheel turns the opposite direction from the wheels it is touching. Wheel A is being turned clockwise by a force as shown. What direction is wheel C turning?

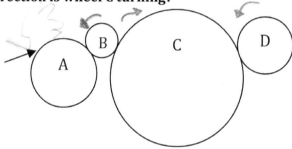

    a. Wheel C does not turn at all because it is too much larger than wheel B
    b. Wheel C does not turn at all because it is not touching wheel B
    c. Wheel C turns counterclockwise
    d. Wheel C turns clockwise

29. Water is stored underground, as well as in oceans and ice caps. Such underground storage reservoirs are called:

    a. Storage tanks
    b. Aquifers
    c. Evaporators
    d. Runoff

30. An ice cube tray is filled with water. The tray is placed in a freezer for 12 hours. The water freezes forming ice. The tray is removed from the freezer and left on a counter for 12 hours. What changes as the water becomes ice and then melts back into water?

    a. The amount of energy in the water
    b. The amount of water in the ice cube tray
    c. The number of water molecules
    d. The mass of the water molecules

31. Several people were asked to jump on a large trampoline, one at a time, to see who could jump the highest. The results were recorded in the data table below.

Person	Weight	Highest Jump
Sarah	59 kg	1.35 m
Mark	75 kg	1.81 m
Isaac	78 kg	1.93 m
Valerie	64 kg	1.47 m
Crystal	66 kg	1.57 m

Based on the data, what can be concluded about the relationship between weight and jumping height?

    a. The more a person weighs, the higher he or she could jump
    b. The less a person weighs, the higher he or she could jump
    c. A person's weight does not affect how high he or she was able to jump
    d. The taller the person is, the higher he or she could jump

32. Which statement describes how Earth's relationship to the Sun allows the polar ice caps to remain frozen?

    a. The equator receives the most direct sunlight while the poles receive the least amount of sunlight
    b. The Moon reflects the Sun's light away from the North and South Pole preventing them from heating up
    c. Wind currents constantly move air warmed by the Sun away from the North and South Pole and toward the equator
    d. The Sun does not shine on the North or South Pole so they never warm up

33. A Tsunami may be caused by:

    a. Earthquakes
    b. Volcanoes
    c. Landslides
    d. A, B, and C

34. Which piece of safety equipment is designed to protect your eyes?

    a. Glasses
    b. Goggles
    c. Gloves
    d. Eye wash

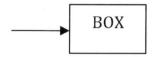

35. How is force being applied to the box below?

$\longrightarrow$ | BOX |

a. The box is being pulled forward
b. The box is being pushed forward
c. Gravity is forcing the box to move forward
d. Friction is forcing the box to stop

36. Your teacher gives you a beaker of water and a beaker of vinegar. Both liquids are clear. What is the best way to distinguish between the two liquids?

a. Take a small sip of each liquid, the vinegar will taste bad
b. Put your nose directly over each beaker and inhale deeply, the vinegar will smell bad
c. Add some baking soda to each beaker, the vinegar will react and form bubbles
d. Ask your teacher to label the beakers before handing them to you

37. Which of the following does not represent a physical change?

a. Salt dissolved in water
b. A spoiling apple
c. Sand dissolved in water
d. Pulverized rock

38. Polar bears, seals and walrus' are all arctic animals that have a thick layer of blubber or fat beneath their skin. What purpose does this layer of blubber serve?

a. Protects them from predators
b. Helps to preserve body heat
c. Aids in finding food
d. Prevents them from drowning in water

39. What does not need to be done after performing an experiment?

a. Wash hands
b. Brush hair
c. Clean up area
d. Complete the lab assignment

40. Why do some cacti have folds in their outer skin?

a. The folds can expand, allowing the cacti to absorb and store water when it rains
b. The folds help protect the cacti from predators
c. The folds allow them to absorb nutrients from the air
d. The folds provide support, allowing the cacti to grow tall

fold = thorn

41. The factor most responsible for determining which season an area is experiencing is

a. Elevation
b. The position of the earth in its orbit around the sun
c. Latitude
d. Air masses

42. After a science laboratory exercise, some solutions remain unused and are left over. What should be done with these solutions?

    a. Dispose of the solutions according to local disposal procedures
    b. Empty the solutions into the sink and rinse with warm water and soap
    c. Ensure the solutions are secured in closed containers and throw away
    d. Store the solutions in a secured, dry place for later use

43. Compared to fresh water, the freezing point of sea water is

    a. Higher
    b. Lower
    c. About the same
    d. Sea water does not freeze

44. Which of the following processes is NOT part of the formation of sedimentary rock?

    a. Layering
    b. Cementation
    c. Compaction
    d. Heat

Answers and Explanations

1. A: In the ecosystem described, birds eat beetles, crickets, and grasshoppers. If a pesticide were to kill off part of the beetle population, birds would be forced to consume more crickets and grasshoppers to meet their energy needs. As a result, there would be a decrease in the cricket population.

2. B: Herbivores are organisms that eat producers (plants) only. In the ecosystem described, both grasshoppers and crickets are herbivores, eating corn and grass.

3. A: Animals breathe in oxygen and breathe out carbon dioxide in a process called respiration. Plants use the carbon dioxide that animals exhale, in the process of photosynthesis, and convert it into oxygen.

4. A: Earth sits on its axis at a tilt of 23.4°. Choice B would result in Earth rotating sideways and choice C is straight up and down. Choice D is not even physically possible.

5. A: A hypothesis is an educated guess formulated by the experimenter based on prior experiments and research. A hypothesis includes what the experimenters think is going to happen and their reasoning.

6. B: Tides are caused by the effect of the Moon's gravity and the Sun's gravity pulling on the ocean waters.

7. B: A year is determined by the number of days it takes for a body to make one revolution around the Sun. So a Martian year would be the number of days it takes for Mars to orbit the Sun.

8. A: A food chain shows how energy flows from one consumer to another. The arrows point in the direction that energy moves. For example, if an arrow points from a flower to a bee, then the energy from the flower flows to the bee as the bee eats the nectar of the flower.

9. A: Lions live in a wide open area where there are few large objects to hide behind. In order to get close enough to their prey to chase and attack it, they must be able to sneak up on it. Their coloration is similar to the color of the tall grasses where they live. This allows the lions to blend into their surroundings and get close to their prey.

10. B: When Mario lets go of the book, he is no longer exerting any force on it, so he cannot be doing work on it. In all the other examples, Mario is exerting a force on the book in the direction that it is moving. In Answer A, Mario moves a book from the floor to the top shelf. Mario lifted up vertically on the book, in the same direction that the book moved, so he was doing work. In Answer C, Mario pushes a box of books across the room. This is also an example of work being done because the box moved in the direction of the force Mario applied. In Answer D, Mario is indirectly applying a horizontal force to the book because of the friction between the book and his head, so he is exerting a force on the book in the direction he is moving.

11. C: Wind farms harvest energy from wind to use in combination with or in place of fossil fuels. The biggest limiting factors for wind farms are the inconsistency and unpredictability of wind and the difficulties involved in storing the energy that has been harvested. Wind farms can only produce as much energy as they receive from wind.

12. B: Carnivores eat meat only. The only choice that is not meat is acorns, which are plant products.

13. C: In this case, the term "how long" refers to the time it takes to do something, such as how long it takes a boy to run 100 meters. The instrument to measure time is a stopwatch.

14. A: To be the more precise, the students could complete the lab again. In fact, all scientific laws have been developed by being tested over and over again through repetitive scientific experiment.

15. B: A cooking pot must be able to conduct heat from the stove into the food being prepared. The only material that is a conductor from the choices given is copper.

16. C: Flowers, trees, and shrubs are all plants, which are producers. Producers are able to make their own food using energy from the Sun in a process known as photosynthesis.

17. B: A mirror is a reflective surface. The flat shiny surface reflects any incoming light allowing a person standing in front of the mirror to see their reflection.

18. A: Tropical environments typically receive rain 5 to 6 times per week, even if it is only a brief afternoon shower. In its new environment the tropical plant is not receiving enough water to survive.

19. There are eight planets in our solar system: Mercury, Venus, Earth, Mars, Jupiter, Saturn, Uranus, and Neptune.

20. C: Pluto was originally classified as a planet but in 2006, it was changed to a dwarf planet because of other similar type objects orbiting very close to it.

21. B: Algae are a type of plant that grows in water. Because algae are plants they are able to capture light from the Sun and transform it into energy during the process of photosynthesis.

22. B: A variable is something that is changed in the experiment. It is being tested against other similar things. In this experiment, the variable is the type of window cleaner.

23. B: The empty shopping cart does not weigh very much and is easy to push. As groceries are added to the empty cart, the cart gains mass. By the time the shopping cart is full, it has more mass than it began with and requires more force to push it.

24. D: The table states that a person's mass remains the same, but weight will fluctuate with the force of gravity. It also states that the more gravity acting on an object, the more the object will weigh. Neptune has a greater gravitational force than Earth, so the person's weight would increase.

25. B: The spring has a length of 1 cm before the force, and a length of 1.5 cm afterwards. The difference in lengths is 0.5 cm.

26. C: The table shows that the largest dogs have the lowest pitch barks ranging from 8 to 12 hertz. The smaller dogs, such as the Chihuahua and spaniel, have higher pitch barks of 17 and 14 hertz.

27. A: The Moon does not emit any light of its own. However, the Moon does reflect light from the Sun. The phase of the Moon that we are able to see on Earth, such as full moon, crescent, or no moon, depends on where the Moon is positioned in relation to the Sun and Earth.

28. D: Wheel A is turning clockwise, which causes wheel B to turn counterclockwise. Wheel B then causes wheel C to turn clockwise. The question states that the wheels are in contact, and while wheel C's size will cause it to rotate more slowly; it will not prevent it from turning.

29. B: An aquifer (a word derived from the Latin root *aqua*, meaning water) is any geologic formation containing ground water.

30. A: When water changes from a liquid to a solid the amount of thermal energy is decreasing. The molecules move closer together, which creates the solid crystal structure of the ice. As the ice melts back into a liquid, thermal energy level increases, causing the molecules to spread out again.

31. A: The table shows a clear correlation between mass and jump height. If you put the list of jumpers in order from highest mass to lowest mass, they will also be in order from highest jump height to lowest jump height. Choice D can be eliminated immediately because there is no information about any of the individuals' heights in the data table or in the question.

32. A: The equator receives the most direct sunlight while the North and South Pole receive the least amount of direct sunlight. In addition, the atmosphere helps to reflect some of the Sun's heat energy away from the poles. Finally, the reflectivity of the ice helps to deflect some of the heat away from the polar ice caps.

33. D: A tsunami, sometimes referred to as a tidal wave, is a large wave or series of waves caused by the displacement of a large volume of water. While the most common cause is an earthquake, large landslides (either falling into the sea or taking place under water) or explosive volcanic action may also result in a tsunami. Tsunamis take the appearance of very high, sustained tides, and may move water very far inland. Large storms, such as cyclones or hurricanes, may also displace great quantities of water, causing a high tide known as a storm surge that also resembles a tsunami.

34. B: Goggles are proper protective eyewear for laboratory. Glasses provide almost no protection as they could break and they are open around the sides where chemicals could splash into the eyes. An eye wash is used to rinse out eyes if chemicals accidently get splashed into them.

35. B: The picture shows an arrow behind the box pushing it forward. If the box were being pulled, the arrow would be in front of the box pulling the box forward. Gravity pulls downward, not forward.

36. D: Labeling beakers before adding fluids to them helps to ensure that the fluids are placed in correct containers and can be identified after being poured. Smelling, tasting, and adding chemicals other than those directed by your instructor are a violation of lab safety.

37. B: A spoiling apple has undergone a chemical change (one substance is changed into another). Dissolving both sand and salt in water, refers to a physical change, since the salt and water and the sand and water can be separated again by evaporating the water, which is a physical change. Pulverized rock is also an example of a physical change where the form has changed but not the substance itself.

38. B: Polar bears, seals, and walrus' all live in arctic climates where it is very cold all year round. The thick layer of blubber that these animals have below the surface of their skin helps them preserve body heat keeping them warm in the frigid environment.

39. B: Brushing hair is not a requirement after completing a laboratory assignment. Choice A, washing hands is required after every lab experiment in order to ensure that no chemicals or lab agents are ingested. Cleaning up the lab area ensures that all equipment is ready for the next experiment. Finishing the assignment is also necessary in order to draw a conclusion from the data collected.

40. A: Cacti live in a desert environment where water is scarce. When it rains, cacti must be able to absorb and store as much water as possible so that they have water available during the dry periods. The folds on the outside of a cactus allow it to expand and fill with water. After a heavy rain, cacti will appear round and plump because the folds are full of water.

41. B: As the earth travels around the sun, it tilts towards the sun or away from it, depending on where it is in its orbit. This tilt is what determines the seasons. The earth is tilted towards the sun in summer and away from it in winter. Elevation a. and latitude c. of an area remain constant throughout the year, so they cannot account for the changing of the seasons. Air masses d. can influence the weather, but don't determine the seasons.

42. A: Dispose of the solutions according to local disposal procedures. Solutions and compounds used in labs may be hazardous according to state and local regulatory agencies and should be treated with such precaution. Answer B, Empty the solutions into the sink and rinse with warm water and soap, does not take into account the hazards associated with a specific solution in terms of vapors, or interactions with water, soap and waste piping systems. Answer C, Ensure the solutions are secured in closed containers and throw away, may allow toxic chemicals to get into landfills and subsequently into fresh water systems. Answer D, Store the solutions in a secured, dry place for later use, is incorrect as chemicals should not be re-used due to the possibility of contamination.

43. B: The freezing point of sea water is lower than fresh water as sea water is more dense. It is more dense because it has more dissolved salts. The freezing point changes with salinity, pressure and density, but can be -2°C (28.4°F) compared with fresh water, 0°C (32°F). As sea water freezes, it forms pockets of high-salinity brine that do not freeze. The brine slowly leaches out of the sea water ice as it forms. When the ice eventually melts, it has a lesser degree of salinity.

44. D: The formation of sedimentary rock does not include heat. Of the three types of rock igneous, sedimentary and metamorphic, heat is essential to two: igneous and metamorphic. Sedimentary rocks are formed by sediments that get deposited and then compacted or cemented together. Sedimentary rocks are classified into detrital, organic or chemical sediments. Answer A, layering, is correct since sediments can be deposited or otherwise formed in layers. Answer B, cementation, is also called lithification. Answer C, compaction, refers to the pressure forming sedimentary rock leading to cementation.

How to Overcome Test Anxiety

Just the thought of taking a test is enough to make most people a little nervous. A test is an important event that can have a long-term impact on your future, so it's important to take it seriously and it's natural to feel anxious about performing well. But just because anxiety is normal, that doesn't mean that it's helpful in test taking, or that you should simply accept it as part of your life. Anxiety can have a variety of effects. These effects can be mild, like making you feel slightly nervous, or severe, like blocking your ability to focus or remember even a simple detail.

If you experience test anxiety—whether severe or mild—it's important to know how to beat it. To discover this, first you need to understand what causes test anxiety.

Causes of Test Anxiety

While we often think of anxiety as an uncontrollable emotional state, it can actually be caused by simple, practical things. One of the most common causes of test anxiety is that a person does not feel adequately prepared for their test. This feeling can be the result of many different issues such as poor study habits or lack of organization, but the most common culprit is time management. Starting to study too late, failing to organize your study time to cover all of the material, or being distracted while you study will mean that you're not well prepared for the test. This may lead to cramming the night before, which will cause you to be physically and mentally exhausted for the test. Poor time management also contributes to feelings of stress, fear, and hopelessness as you realize you are not well prepared but don't know what to do about it.

Other times, test anxiety is not related to your preparation for the test but comes from unresolved fear. This may be a past failure on a test, or poor performance on tests in general. It may come from comparing yourself to others who seem to be performing better or from the stress of living up to expectations. Anxiety may be driven by fears of the future—how failure on this test would affect your educational and career goals. These fears are often completely irrational, but they can still negatively impact your test performance.

> **Review Video: 3 Reasons You Have Test Anxiety**
> Visit mometrix.com/academy and enter code: 428468

Elements of Test Anxiety

As mentioned earlier, test anxiety is considered to be an emotional state, but it has physical and mental components as well. Sometimes you may not even realize that you are suffering from test anxiety until you notice the physical symptoms. These can include trembling hands, rapid heartbeat, sweating, nausea, and tense muscles. Extreme anxiety may lead to fainting or vomiting. Obviously, any of these symptoms can have a negative impact on testing. It is important to recognize them as soon as they begin to occur so that you can address the problem before it damages your performance.

> **Review Video: 3 Ways to Tell You Have Test Anxiety**
> Visit mometrix.com/academy and enter code: 927847

The mental components of test anxiety include trouble focusing and inability to remember learned information. During a test, your mind is on high alert, which can help you recall information and stay focused for an extended period of time. However, anxiety interferes with your mind's natural processes, causing you to blank out, even on the questions you know well. The strain of testing during anxiety makes it difficult to stay focused, especially on a test that may take several hours. Extreme anxiety can take a huge mental toll, making it difficult not only to recall test information but even to understand the test questions or pull your thoughts together.

> **Review Video: How Test Anxiety Affects Memory**
> Visit mometrix.com/academy and enter code: 609003

Effects of Test Anxiety

Test anxiety is like a disease—if left untreated, it will get progressively worse. Anxiety leads to poor performance, and this reinforces the feelings of fear and failure, which in turn lead to poor performances on subsequent tests. It can grow from a mild nervousness to a crippling condition. If allowed to progress, test anxiety can have a big impact on your schooling, and consequently on your future.

Test anxiety can spread to other parts of your life. Anxiety on tests can become anxiety in any stressful situation, and blanking on a test can turn into panicking in a job situation. But fortunately, you don't have to let anxiety rule your testing and determine your grades. There are a number of relatively simple steps you can take to move past anxiety and function normally on a test and in the rest of life.

> **Review Video: How Test Anxiety Impacts Your Grades**
> Visit mometrix.com/academy and enter code: 939819

Physical Steps for Beating Test Anxiety

While test anxiety is a serious problem, the good news is that it can be overcome. It doesn't have to control your ability to think and remember information. While it may take time, you can begin taking steps today to beat anxiety.

Just as your first hint that you may be struggling with anxiety comes from the physical symptoms, the first step to treating it is also physical. Rest is crucial for having a clear, strong mind. If you are tired, it is much easier to give in to anxiety. But if you establish good sleep habits, your body and mind will be ready to perform optimally, without the strain of exhaustion. Additionally, sleeping well helps you to retain information better, so you're more likely to recall the answers when you see the test questions.

Getting good sleep means more than going to bed on time. It's important to allow your brain time to relax. Take study breaks from time to time so it doesn't get overworked, and don't study right before bed. Take time to rest your mind before trying to rest your body, or you may find it difficult to fall asleep.

> **Review Video: <u>The Importance of Sleep for Your Brain</u>**
> Visit mometrix.com/academy and enter code: 319338

Along with sleep, other aspects of physical health are important in preparing for a test. Good nutrition is vital for good brain function. Sugary foods and drinks may give a burst of energy but this burst is followed by a crash, both physically and emotionally. Instead, fuel your body with protein and vitamin-rich foods.

Also, drink plenty of water. Dehydration can lead to headaches and exhaustion, especially if your brain is already under stress from the rigors of the test. Particularly if your test is a long one, drink water during the breaks. And if possible, take an energy-boosting snack to eat between sections.

> **Review Video: <u>How Diet Can Affect your Mood</u>**
> Visit mometrix.com/academy and enter code: 624317

Along with sleep and diet, a third important part of physical health is exercise. Maintaining a steady workout schedule is helpful, but even taking 5-minute study breaks to walk can help get your blood pumping faster and clear your head. Exercise also releases endorphins, which contribute to a positive feeling and can help combat test anxiety.

When you nurture your physical health, you are also contributing to your mental health. If your body is healthy, your mind is much more likely to be healthy as well. So take time to rest, nourish your body with healthy food and water, and get moving as much as possible. Taking these physical steps will make you stronger and more able to take the mental steps necessary to overcome test anxiety.

Mental Steps for Beating Test Anxiety

Working on the mental side of test anxiety can be more challenging, but as with the physical side, there are clear steps you can take to overcome it. As mentioned earlier, test anxiety often stems from lack of preparation, so the obvious solution is to prepare for the test. Effective studying may be the most important weapon you have for beating test anxiety, but you can and should employ several other mental tools to combat fear.

First, boost your confidence by reminding yourself of past success—tests or projects that you aced. If you're putting as much effort into preparing for this test as you did for those, there's no reason you should expect to fail here. Work hard to prepare; then trust your preparation.

Second, surround yourself with encouraging people. It can be helpful to find a study group, but be sure that the people you're around will encourage a positive attitude. If you spend time with others who are anxious or cynical, this will only contribute to your own anxiety. Look for others who are motivated to study hard from a desire to succeed, not from a fear of failure.

Third, reward yourself. A test is physically and mentally tiring, even without anxiety, and it can be helpful to have something to look forward to. Plan an activity following the test, regardless of the outcome, such as going to a movie or getting ice cream.

When you are taking the test, if you find yourself beginning to feel anxious, remind yourself that you know the material. Visualize successfully completing the test. Then take a few deep, relaxing breaths and return to it. Work through the questions carefully but with confidence, knowing that you are capable of succeeding.

Developing a healthy mental approach to test taking will also aid in other areas of life. Test anxiety affects more than just the actual test—it can be damaging to your mental health and even contribute to depression. It's important to beat test anxiety before it becomes a problem for more than testing.

> **Review Video: <u>Test Anxiety and Depression</u>**
> Visit mometrix.com/academy and enter code: 904704

Study Strategy

Being prepared for the test is necessary to combat anxiety, but what does being prepared look like? You may study for hours on end and still not feel prepared. What you need is a strategy for test prep. The next few pages outline our recommended steps to help you plan out and conquer the challenge of preparation.

STEP 1: SCOPE OUT THE TEST

Learn everything you can about the format (multiple choice, essay, etc.) and what will be on the test. Gather any study materials, course outlines, or sample exams that may be available. Not only will this help you to prepare, but knowing what to expect can help to alleviate test anxiety.

STEP 2: MAP OUT THE MATERIAL

Look through the textbook or study guide and make note of how many chapters or sections it has. Then divide these over the time you have. For example, if a book has 15 chapters and you have five days to study, you need to cover three chapters each day. Even better, if you have the time, leave an extra day at the end for overall review after you have gone through the material in depth.

If time is limited, you may need to prioritize the material. Look through it and make note of which sections you think you already have a good grasp on, and which need review. While you are studying, skim quickly through the familiar sections and take more time on the challenging parts. Write out your plan so you don't get lost as you go. Having a written plan also helps you feel more in control of the study, so anxiety is less likely to arise from feeling overwhelmed at the amount to cover.

STEP 3: GATHER YOUR TOOLS

Decide what study method works best for you. Do you prefer to highlight in the book as you study and then go back over the highlighted portions? Or do you type out notes of the important information? Or is it helpful to make flashcards that you can carry with you? Assemble the pens, index cards, highlighters, post-it notes, and any other materials you may need so you won't be distracted by getting up to find things while you study.

If you're having a hard time retaining the information or organizing your notes, experiment with different methods. For example, try color-coding by subject with colored pens, highlighters, or post-it notes. If you learn better by hearing, try recording yourself reading your notes so you can listen while in the car, working out, or simply sitting at your desk. Ask a friend to quiz you from your flashcards, or try teaching someone the material to solidify it in your mind.

STEP 4: CREATE YOUR ENVIRONMENT

It's important to avoid distractions while you study. This includes both the obvious distractions like visitors and the subtle distractions like an uncomfortable chair (or a too-comfortable couch that makes you want to fall asleep). Set up the best study environment possible: good lighting and a comfortable work area. If background music helps you focus, you may want to turn it on, but otherwise keep the room quiet. If you are using a computer to take notes, be sure you don't have any other windows open, especially applications like social media, games, or anything else that could distract you. Silence your phone and turn off notifications. Be sure to keep water close by so you stay hydrated while you study (but avoid unhealthy drinks and snacks).

Also, take into account the best time of day to study. Are you freshest first thing in the morning? Try to set aside some time then to work through the material. Is your mind clearer in the afternoon or evening? Schedule your study session then. Another method is to study at the same time of day that you will take the test, so that your brain gets used to working on the material at that time and will be ready to focus at test time.

STEP 5: STUDY!

Once you have done all the study preparation, it's time to settle into the actual studying. Sit down, take a few moments to settle your mind so you can focus, and begin to follow your study plan. Don't give in to distractions or let yourself procrastinate. This is your time to prepare so you'll be ready to fearlessly approach the test. Make the most of the time and stay focused.

Of course, you don't want to burn out. If you study too long you may find that you're not retaining the information very well. Take regular study breaks. For example, taking five minutes out of every hour to walk briskly, breathing deeply and swinging your arms, can help your mind stay fresh.

As you get to the end of each chapter or section, it's a good idea to do a quick review. Remind yourself of what you learned and work on any difficult parts. When you feel that you've mastered the material, move on to the next part. At the end of your study session, briefly skim through your notes again.

But while review is helpful, cramming last minute is NOT. If at all possible, work ahead so that you won't need to fit all your study into the last day. Cramming overloads your brain with more information than it can process and retain, and your tired mind may struggle to recall even previously learned information when it is overwhelmed with last-minute study. Also, the urgent nature of cramming and the stress placed on your brain contribute to anxiety. You'll be more likely to go to the test feeling unprepared and having trouble thinking clearly.

So don't cram, and don't stay up late before the test, even just to review your notes at a leisurely pace. Your brain needs rest more than it needs to go over the information again. In fact, plan to finish your studies by noon or early afternoon the day before the test. Give your brain the rest of the day to relax or focus on other things, and get a good night's sleep. Then you will be fresh for the test and better able to recall what you've studied.

STEP 6: TAKE A PRACTICE TEST

Many courses offer sample tests, either online or in the study materials. This is an excellent resource to check whether you have mastered the material, as well as to prepare for the test format and environment.

Check the test format ahead of time: the number of questions, the type (multiple choice, free response, etc.), and the time limit. Then create a plan for working through them. For example, if you have 30 minutes to take a 60-question test, your limit is 30 seconds per question. Spend less time on the questions you know well so that you can take more time on the difficult ones.

If you have time to take several practice tests, take the first one open book, with no time limit. Work through the questions at your own pace and make sure you fully understand them. Gradually work up to taking a test under test conditions: sit at a desk with all study materials put away and set a timer. Pace yourself to make sure you finish the test with time to spare and go back to check your answers if you have time.

After each test, check your answers. On the questions you missed, be sure you understand why you missed them. Did you misread the question (tests can use tricky wording)? Did you forget the information? Or was it something you hadn't learned? Go back and study any shaky areas that the practice tests reveal.

Taking these tests not only helps with your grade, but also aids in combating test anxiety. If you're already used to the test conditions, you're less likely to worry about it, and working through tests until you're scoring well gives you a confidence boost. Go through the practice tests until you feel comfortable, and then you can go into the test knowing that you're ready for it.

Test Tips

On test day, you should be confident, knowing that you've prepared well and are ready to answer the questions. But aside from preparation, there are several test day strategies you can employ to maximize your performance.

First, as stated before, get a good night's sleep the night before the test (and for several nights before that, if possible). Go into the test with a fresh, alert mind rather than staying up late to study.

Try not to change too much about your normal routine on the day of the test. It's important to eat a nutritious breakfast, but if you normally don't eat breakfast at all, consider eating just a protein bar. If you're a coffee drinker, go ahead and have your normal coffee. Just make sure you time it so that the caffeine doesn't wear off right in the middle of your test. Avoid sugary beverages, and drink enough water to stay hydrated but not so much that you need a restroom break 10 minutes into the test. If your test isn't first thing in the morning, consider going for a walk or doing a light workout before the test to get your blood flowing.

Allow yourself enough time to get ready, and leave for the test with plenty of time to spare so you won't have the anxiety of scrambling to arrive in time. Another reason to be early is to select a good seat. It's helpful to sit away from doors and windows, which can be distracting. Find a good seat, get out your supplies, and settle your mind before the test begins.

When the test begins, start by going over the instructions carefully, even if you already know what to expect. Make sure you avoid any careless mistakes by following the directions.

Then begin working through the questions, pacing yourself as you've practiced. If you're not sure on an answer, don't spend too much time on it, and don't let it shake your confidence. Either skip it and come back later, or eliminate as many wrong answers as possible and guess among the remaining ones. Don't dwell on these questions as you continue—put them out of your mind and focus on what lies ahead.

Be sure to read all of the answer choices, even if you're sure the first one is the right answer. Sometimes you'll find a better one if you keep reading. But don't second-guess yourself if you do immediately know the answer. Your gut instinct is usually right. Don't let test anxiety rob you of the information you know.

If you have time at the end of the test (and if the test format allows), go back and review your answers. Be cautious about changing any, since your first instinct tends to be correct, but make sure you didn't misread any of the questions or accidentally mark the wrong answer choice. Look over any you skipped and make an educated guess.

At the end, leave the test feeling confident. You've done your best, so don't waste time worrying about your performance or wishing you could change anything. Instead, celebrate the successful completion of this test. And finally, use this test to learn how to deal with anxiety even better next time.

> **Review Video: 5 Tips to Beat Test Anxiety**
> Visit mometrix.com/academy and enter code: 570656

Important Qualification

Not all anxiety is created equal. If your test anxiety is causing major issues in your life beyond the classroom or testing center, or if you are experiencing troubling physical symptoms related to your anxiety, it may be a sign of a serious physiological or psychological condition. If this sounds like your situation, we strongly encourage you to seek professional help.

Thank You

We at Mometrix would like to extend our heartfelt thanks to you, our friend and patron, for allowing us to play a part in your journey. It is a privilege to serve people from all walks of life who are unified in their commitment to building the best future they can for themselves.

The preparation you devote to these important testing milestones may be the most valuable educational opportunity you have for making a real difference in your life. We encourage you to put your heart into it—that feeling of succeeding, overcoming, and yes, conquering will be well worth the hours you've invested.

We want to hear your story, your struggles and your successes, and if you see any opportunities for us to improve our materials so we can help others even more effectively in the future, please share that with us as well. **The team at Mometrix would be absolutely thrilled to hear from you!** So please, send us an email (support@mometrix.com) and let's stay in touch.

If you'd like some additional help, check out these other resources we offer for your exam:

http://MometrixFlashcards.com/CaliforniaStandardsTests

Additional Bonus Material

Due to our efforts to try to keep this book to a manageable length, we've created a link that will give you access to all of your additional bonus material.

Please visit http://www.mometrix.com/bonus948/cstg5sci to access the information.